To David & Sara
with gratitude for your ministry (s)
Grace in Christ,
Allen

Fruit-full Living

A Guide for Growing In God's Spirit

Allen R. Hunt

SPG SELAH PUBLISHING GROUP

Publishing services by Selah Publishing Group, LLC, Arizona. The views expressed or implied in this work do not necessarily reflect those of Selah Publishing Group.

Unless otherwise noted scripture references are translated by Allen R. Hunt from the Greek and Hebrew texts of scripture.

Scripture quotations marked (NIV) are taken from the HOLY BIBLE, NEW INTERNATIONAL VERSION®.

Scripture quotations marked (NRSV) are from the New Revised Standard Version Bible, copyright 1989 by the Division of Christian Education of the National Council of the Churches of Christ in the U.S.A. Used by permission. All rights reserved.

ISBN 1-58930-073-4
Library of Congress Control Number: 2002112995

To the girls at Orange and Canner.
They are God's greatest blessing to me.

Contents

Acknowledgments

I have been blessed by God in many ways: with good friends, good family, and good teachers. There is no possible way to thank all of the persons who have helped to make this book—as well as my ministry—possible.

However, it is important to specifically thank a handful of people:

1. The congregations of New Hope, Hamden Plains, Chapel Hill, and Mount Pisgah. I thank God for you all.

2. Brunner and Pat Hunt; Ray and Jerry Ann Griffin. Greater parents do not exist.

3. Teachers: Wayne Meeks, Fred Craddock, Carl Holladay, Abe Malherbe, Wayne Mixon, Sonya Lyda, and Clara Hirschfield. I have never had an original idea, and much of anything valuable here originated with good teachers like these.

4. Colleagues: Mike Reinsel, Steven Boguslawski, O.P., Andy Stanley, Beth Barnwell, David and Alice Hubbell, and Sheri Browne, all of whom helped in very real and tangible ways.

Lastly, let me say that the examples used are from real lives, unless otherwise noted. With the exception of persons portrayed in the publications, I have changed the names and some details in order to protect their privacy. I have also tried to acknowledge, without being too cumbersome, any external major sources of material. In addition, it is important to note that all translations of the Bible contained herein are my own. Any errors, also, are my own.

Fruit-full Living

"...the fruit of the Spirit is love, joy, peace, patience, kindness, goodness, faithfulness, gentleness, self-control..."
Galatians 5:22—23a

Introduction

Very simply, life in Jesus makes us new. With faith comes the gift of the Holy Spirit in our lives and the gift of a new life. In that new life, Jesus slowly puts to death the sinful impulses and desires in each of us. Things that once were important to us no longer are. We have changed. No, we have *been* changed. Changed by God. Changed by Jesus. Changed by God's Holy Spirit. Our passions for the works of the flesh fade into the background as Jesus brings forth new fruit. The apostle Paul describes that fruit as "the fruit of the Spirit." In Galatians 5:22-23, he lists nine of these: love, joy, peace, patience, kindness, goodness, faithfulness, gentleness, and self-control.

These nine fruit of God's Spirit are the focus of this book. They blossom in our lives as we grow in Jesus and in the faith. As He changes our lives and reshapes our hearts, these fruit are the evidence of His work in us. Thus, it is important to know more about these qualities that God wants to see in each of our lives. As they are cultivated, we begin to become the person God desires us to be and the person He created us to be.

Notice that Paul says "*fruit* of the Spirit" rather than "*fruits*," using the singular not the plural. He does this because God does not give us just one or a few of the fruit as His children. No, He begins to bring *all* of these fruit to reality in our lives when we become Christians. That is the work of the Holy Spirit in us.

As the Spirit works in us, we not only become more loving, we also grow more patient. We not only begin to experience peace, we become faithful. These fruit may grow at different rates and at different times in our spiritual lives, but each Christian can and will experience growth in all of them to some degree. In this way, the fruit of the Spirit are not like spiritual gifts with which God endows each Christian (e.g., prophecy, leadership, evangelism, and so on). But God endows each Christian with some measure of *all* of the fruit of His Spirit. In other words, when we live in the Spirit of God, we will all begin to see love, joy, peace, patience, kindness, goodness, faithfulness, gentleness, and self-control blossom in our lives. That is how the world will know that we belong to Jesus: by the evidence of His fruit in our lives!

It is also important to observe how the final fruit, self-control, can act as a stimulus for the other fruit. When we focus positively on self-control, we soon discover that the other fruit blossom more. By freely exercising our self-contol, we help cultivate the other fruit. In fact, some readers have chosen to begin with Chapter 9 of this book to find ways to help cultivate more fruit in their spiritual lives.

In the following pages, I examine each fruit of the Spirit. Each chapter takes a look at what that spiritual fruit really looks like. In addition, I show you examples from the Bible for each fruit and try to help you understand what God is doing in the heart of the believer. I also provide examples from real-life events. My goal is not only to grow your biblical understanding of each of these fruit but to provide practical tips that you can use to allow these fruit to blossom in your life. God desires for you to be fruitful, fruit-filled, and fruit-full. At the end of the chapters, I have provided more than sixty ways to increase your "fruit-full-ness."

Jesus invites us to a special life-changing journey, the journey of faith. As we meet and encounter Him, and as we grow in the faith that He provides, Jesus begins His work of transforming our lives. We become new people. As Galatians 3.26 reminds us, we are now "children of God." That's good news!

In his letter to the Galatians, the apostle Paul describes this new life in Jesus in some unique and exciting ways. He writes in Galatians 2:19-20,

> I have been crucified with Christ; and it is no longer I who live, but Christ who lives in me. And the life I now live in the flesh, I live by faith in the Son of God, who loved me and gave Himself up for me. (NRSV)

What Paul describes here is a revolutionary idea: when we have faith in Jesus as our Lord, He begins at that moment to live within us. We can and will never be the same again. But that is only the beginning. When Jesus lives in the believer's heart, we each live a new and different life. And that life is filled with the fruit of God's Spirit.

This means we are new and different. As children of God, we no longer live by the world's values and standards; instead, we live by faith in the Son of God. A Christian's values differ from the values we see in the world. Where the world sees nothing but opportunity for personal wealth and fame, the Christian sees opportunity for service and humility. When the world says, "If it feels good, do it," Jesus says, "Deny yourself and follow me." When the world says, "I gotta be me," Jesus says, "You are my sheep, my flock." When the world says. "Do unto others, and then split," Jesus says, "Do unto others as you would have them do unto you." *To follow Jesus is to be different.* To have Jesus in the heart is to be a new and different person. We become new people.

Rather than embracing the passions and desires of the world, children of God live by faith in the Son of God, embrace His ways, and bear His fruit. In other words, Jesus takes control of our hearts, and He frees us from the awful bondage of serving only ourselves and of seeking only our own advantage in all that we do. He liberates us from selfishness and moves us into a holiness that desires nothing but God and His pleasure.

What does this look like? St. Francis of Assisi captures this contrast between Christians and the world in his famous prayer:

> Lord, make me an instrument of your peace;
> where there is hatred, let me sow love;
> where there is injury, pardon;
> where there is doubt, faith;
> where there is despair, hope;
> where there is darkness, light;
> and where there is sadness, joy.
>
> O Divine Master,
> Grant that I may not so much seek
> to be consoled as to console;

to be understood, as to understand,
to be loved as to love;
for it is in giving that we receive,
it is in pardoning that we are pardoned,
And it is in dying that we are born to eternal life.

Again, Christians *are* different. In this prayer, St. Francis contrasts what we often see in the world (hatred, injury, doubt, despair, darkness, and sadness) with the priorities of God (love, pardon, faith, hope, light, and joy). In his own way, St. Francis is sharing the same views that Paul gives us in Galatians 5:16 NRSV when he says, "Live by the Spirit, I say, and do not gratify the desires of the flesh." When we seek to live by faith in God rather than by faith in ourselves or in the powers of this world, our behaviors, values, and priorities change. No more will these works of the flesh control us: sexual immorality, impurity, and debauchery; idolatry and witchcraft; hatred, discord, jealousy, fits of rage, selfish ambition, dissensions, factions, and envy; drunkenness, and orgies (Galatians 5:19-21). These works of the flesh end only in the very things St. Francis wishes to overcome: sadness and despair.

God's alternative is life in the Spirit. God's alternative is fruit, the fruit of His Spirit. Jesus offers that to us. He offers true life; He offers faith; He offers joy. How does that happen? True life really begins when the fruit of God's Holy Spirit begin to grow in our hearts and lives. It is very simple: Jesus changes you and me from the inside out!

I hope that these chapters will make good material for your personal spiritual growth and devotional life. My primary aim is to help you grow in your love for God who desires no more and no less than for your heart to belong to Him. God has promised you the presence of His Spirit and He wants these fruit of the Spirit to prosper in your life. His Son, Jesus, has assured you that He lives within you. Turn that knowledge loose in how you live. Live fruit-fully!

Love

"...the fruit of the Spirit is love, joy, peace, patience, kindness, goodness, faithfulness, gentleness, self-control..."

GALATIANS 5:22—23a

Chapter 1 Love

"...the fruit of the Spirit is *love...*"

Love makes a difference. In recent years, America has witnessed a tragic phenomenon: babies being born either already addicted to drugs or already suffering from deadly diseases such as AIDS. This tragic phenomenon has reached epidemic proportions as thousands of babies are born into the world with the odds stacked drastically against them. With a parent, or parents, addicted or dying, the infant has little external stimulation. The first few weeks of life often present more challenges than the newborn can withstand. With a body ravaged by chemical dependency or deadly disease, the child struggles to stay alive.

In an effort to combat these seemingly insurmountable odds against life, some hospitals and medical teams have created a new strategy. They now recruit volunteers from the community to stop by daily, simply to hold, touch, and interact with these uniquely challenged children. What they have discovered surprises even the most advanced medical researchers. By providing external stimulation and loving care for the infants, the rate of survival dramatically increases. As the volunteers reach out to these tiny humans who receive little or no other family attention, fewer infant deaths can be attributed to "failure to thrive," the medical term for children who never seem to gain momentum in living. Love makes the difference.

It is simple: humans need love. Without it we will die. Failure to thrive really means "failure to be loved."

In the thirteenth century, Frederick II wanted to test babies to discover what language they would speak if they never interacted with adults but only with each other. Would it be Latin or Greek or some other language unknown to adults? To find out, he had a group of infants quarantined—separated from all adults other than a person who silently changed diapers and provided some food each day—only to discover that the isolation caused them to die. Instead of learning what language they developed, Frederick found that without the love of a mother or caring adult, the children could not survive. Failure to thrive. Failure to be loved. Love is essential for our lives.

In the first century, Christians were not the only organized groups in the Roman world. Dinner groups met for social purposes. Burial societies were organized to provide social interaction and provision for post-death arrangements. Philosophical schools created opportunities for persons to gather around one or more gifted teachers for the purpose of pursuing education and intellectual achievement. Pagan cults sought to give meaning to life through their seasonal rituals and sacrifices to the gods.

However, Christians were the only group governed by the principle of love. The apostle Paul describes love as the highest and best spiritual gift to be experienced in this lifetime:

> And I will show you a still more excellent way.
> If I speak in the tongues of men and of angels, but have not *love*, I am a noisy gong or a clanging cymbal. And if I have prophetic powers, and understand all mysteries and all knowledge. and if I have faith, so as to move mountains, but have not *love*, I am nothing. If I give away all that I have, and if I deliver my body to be burned but have not *love*, I gain nothing.

Love is patient and kind; *love* is not jealous or boastful; it is not arrogant or rude. *Love* does not insist on its own way; it is not irritable or resentful; it does not rejoice at wrong, but rejoices in the right. *Love* bears all things, believes all things, hopes all things, endures all things.

Love never ends.

1 CORINTHIANS 12:31–13:8

Jesus tells His disciples that the world will know that they are His followers and His children by their love. "By this all men will know that you are my disciples, if you have love for one another" (John 13:35 NIV).

Clearly, love is important. It is central to what Christians believe and value. But, what is this love, characterized in the original Greek as *agape* love? What does it look like? Where does it come from? How do we obtain this kind of love in our lives?

God's Love for Humans

The Bible is a story of love: God's love for the world and God's love for His children. Nowhere do we see the love of God more active than in Jesus. "For God so *loved* the world that He gave His only begotten Son, that whoever believes in Him should not perish but have eternal life" (John 3:16). This famous verse captures the heart of the Bible, the heart of the gospel, and truly the heart of God. Jesus came to us because God loves us. That is the supreme example of *agape* love. God loves us first. Jesus proves it by giving His life.

In Jesus, we see God taking the first step in touching and shaping the lives of His children. In offering His Son to us, He shows us His highest hopes and dreams for our own lives. He wants us to be like Christ. Jesus represents all that we humans can be. Most of all, because He is willing to sacrifice Himself for us at the cross, Jesus represents love. That's what *agape* love is: self-sacrificial love. *Agape* love thinks of the other person first and is willing to sacrifice in order to help that other person.

Jesus is God's *agape* love. God loves each of us so much that He is willing to sacrifice His own substance, Jesus, His Son, on our behalf. That is the model of love. God loves us first.

God's story of love continues! Jesus issues the invitation to us all: love Him. Hear the words of Jesus: "He who has my commandments and keeps them, is he who *loves* me, and he who *loves* me will be *loved* by my Father, and I will *love* him and manifest myself to him" (John 14: 21). When we obey Jesus, we love Him. Our actions and our service to Him become expressions of our love for Him. And when we love Jesus, we love God.

The news gets even better! When we love Jesus, God in turn loves us and continues to show Himself to us. He is the Source of our strength. God's love flows into our lives and provides a special power that the world cannot give. When we love Jesus, God's love becomes a part of who we are. We only then begin to realize the full potential that He has in mind for us. We start to understand *who* we are. And we also realize *whose* we are. We are God's children. We belong to Him.

As God's children, and as lovers and followers of Jesus, we are invited to live in that love. We become "Jesus People." What a revolutionary way to live! "As the Father has loved me, so have I loved you, abide in my love" (John 15:9 NRSV). Jesus invites us to spend our days and our energies in that love. It then becomes not merely something we feel, or something that we receive; love is where we live. We live in God's love. That is the most special gift of all. Jesus ushers us into a new house of love with Him and the Father above.

Self-help books and self-esteem courses can never replace the most basic knowledge that we belong to God. He loves you and He loves me. That is who you are: a child of God. He has hopes and plans and dreams and goals and visions for your life. God has a blueprint for what He wants you to be. That God-inspired blueprint gives your life meaning, direction, and purpose, and it begins with a simple word: love.

Who are you? *A child loved by God.*

Love is Vertical

Jesus has a lot to say about love. We have already seen that when He instructed His disciples to love one another. Jesus teaches us the basic dimensions and lessons about love. In fact, He says that all of His teaching can be summarized in that one powerful word: *agape*. When He was asked what the greatest teaching or commandment was, Jesus responded, "Love God completely. And love your neighbor as yourself" (Matthew 22:34-40).

The critical importance of *agape* love can best be seen in Jesus' teaching in Mark 12. That may seem like an unlikely place to begin since this chapter shows the many ways in which Jesus disagreed with the Jewish leaders of His time. It is important to remember, however, that Jesus was not always popular. In fact, He often found Himself mired in controversy. Some people loved to fight with Jesus or argue with Him. For example, in the Gospel of Mark alone we find religious authorities, demons, Satan himself, and even occasionally Jesus' own disciples, opposing Him and/or His teachings.

So we should not be surprised to open Mark's chapter 12 and find Jesus in the middle of a series of arguments. One disagreement seems to lead directly to another. Chief priests, scribes, elders, Pharisees, Herodians, and Sadducees parade through the chapter in order to quibble and argue with Jesus over various theological matters. In Mark 12:1-12, Jesus tells the parable of the wicked tenants in the vineyard, and the authorities realize that He "told this parable against them" (12:12) in order to criticize their failure to serve God with their lives. In 12:13-17, Jesus avoids the trap that the authorities seek to set for Him regarding the issue of the payment of taxes. Sadducees question Him regarding the resurrection in 12:18-27, and He denounces the scribes' ostentatious lifestyles in 12:38-40. He reinforces that denunciation with His observation of the supreme value of the widow's offering of a mite in 12:41-44.

However, if we are not careful, we will miss the point of this chapter. In 12:28-34, Jesus and a scribe actually agree. Mark nestles this passage of agreement right after the first three disputes of chapter 12 and just before the final three disputes. In other words, the passage of agreement between Jesus and the religious authorities is located right at the center of chapter 12. This is the heart of chapter 12, and clearly it is the heart of Jesus' teaching. The six stories of disagreement and debate serve only to highlight the focal point of the chapter: 12:28-34. This is the center of the chapter and the center of what binds believers together.

On what, then, do Jesus and the scribe agree? Love. That's it. They both agree that love is the centerpiece of a fruit-full life.

When the scribe asks what is the most important commandment of all, Jesus responds with His famous call to love God entirely with one's heart, soul, mind, and strength as well as to love fully both neighbor and self. Rather than disagreeing with Jesus, the scribe responds, "You are right" (12:32). Given all of the arguments with Jesus, that might sound surprising. The scribe actually agrees with Jesus? Yes.

Why does the scribe agree? Because Jesus' answer simply expands on the basic teachings of the Old Testament found in Leviticus 19 and Deuteronomy 6. God's people are called to love God and love one another. Thus, the scribe and Jesus can agree on this point. Love.

The Old Testament and the New Testament converge with one word: *agape.* Love that sacrifices self in order to love God with abandon and our neighbors with joy. In contrast to all the conflicts in chapter 12 stands the central idea of love—*agape* love.

In order to understand what Jesus is saying, it is important to remember that there were at least three basic kinds of love expressed in the Greek language. Knowing the difference helps us to know how to love God in our lives. *Agape* love is not brotherly love such as we feel for our families and friends. Nor is it erotic love like that between husband and wife. Rather, *agape* love is self-sacrificial love, love that gives, love that considers others first.

Agape love is not a word that Mark throws around lightly in his Gospel. In fact, he only uses the term a few times. He uses this word carefully because, in his mind, God and Jesus are the examples of *agape.* We find the models for how we are to love not in other humans but in the Father and Son.

That means, first, that Jesus teaches us that *agape* love is vertical. Love moves up and down. God's love flows down from above and into our lives. The most significant example of that is in Jesus Himself. God became flesh and lived among us. At Jesus' baptism (Mark 1:9-11) and at His transfiguration on the mountaintop (Mark 9:2-8), Jesus is God's "loved" Son, the one for whom God the Father has *agape* love. Love that gives one's own Son. Hear the words of God the Father: *"This is my Beloved Son."*

When Jesus meets the rich young ruler (Mark 10:17-22), He *loves* him before He says, "You lack one thing; go, sell what you own, and give the money to the poor" (10:21). This is the kind of love that considers the needs of others first and foremost. Jesus loves the young ruler enough to tell him the truth and to invite him to the life God desires for him.

In the parable of the wicked tenants in the vineyard, the master (God, the Father) sends His beloved son (Jesus) into the vineyard only to have him rejected and killed by the tenants. This is self-sacrificial love, love that is willing to suffer on behalf of others. So, when Jesus calls us to lead lives of *agape* love, His call is to imitate the divine example of love that we see in God the Father and Jesus the Son. God loves us first.

But the good news gets even better! God has *agape* love for Jesus just as Jesus has *agape* love for us. God, out of love, sends His beloved Son and offers Him to us. *Agape* is not *part* of the point, it *is* the point. Love is the central point of our relationship with God. He offers His own Son, even to death. The ultimate example of self-giving, self-sacrificing love is the cross. The Cross is love. God loves us first. He has always loved us.

God's old covenant with Israel in the Old Testament finds its completion and fulfillment in the new covenant of Jesus as the two covenants merge in the idea of love, *agape* love. Children of God agree: all you need is love, God's love.

Love is Horizontal

Jesus teaches us that *agape* love also is horizontal. The love that flows down from God above and into our lives is expressed in how we treat other people. Because God has first loved us, He calls us to imitate that love and share it with other people in our lives. That is horizontal love. Love is vertical as we love God above us and His love flows into our lives. Love is horizontal as God's divine love moves out of us into the lives of the other people in our lives and world.

Having *agape* love in our lives means that we will live differently from the rest of the world. "Jesus People" are different. Jesus captures that difference between God's people and the rest of the world in Luke 10:25-37, the parable of the Good Samaritan. You remember the story. A lawyer asks Jesus, "What must I do to inherit eternal life?" Jesus helps the man answer his own question in the same way He Himself answers the scribe in the story we just looked at in Mark 12: with a call to love God and to love our neighbor. But then the scribe asks, "And who is my neighbor?" In other words, what does *agape* love look like in real life? *Agape* love is not just an idea. It can be seen and touched in the real world we live in.

Thus, Jesus shares the marvelous story of the man traveling from Jerusalem to Jericho on a Roman road when he is robbed, stripped, beaten, and left for dead. A priest travels that way, sees the man, and passes by on the other side of the road. Likewise, a Levite holy man does the same thing. However, in a shocking surprise, a Samaritan—an outcast and an alien in the eyes of the Jews—is "moved with pity" (Luke 10:32) and stops to assist the victim of this crime. He bandages the man's wounds, anoints him with oil and wine for the healing of those wounds, and transports the man to an inn where he offers to pay for the man's care and recovery.

Jesus then asks the scribe. "Which of these three men was a neighbor to the man?" The scribe responds, "The one who showed mercy." Then Jesus challenges all of us to "*Go and do* likewise."

Jesus' point is clear: to have the *agape* love of God flowing in our lives means that we show mercy for other people. Why? Not because we are *good*, but because we are *God's!* We love because God first loves us. We show mercy because God first has shown mercy to us. We have *agape* love in our lives only because God has shown His love for us in Jesus. God invites us to share that love generously with the world. We do not act on our own. We act as God's loved children sharing His love with a hurting world.

To share the love of God, or to have *agape* love flowing in our lives, means that we are willing to inconvenience ourselves on behalf of other people. We are willing to sacrifice self for the benefit of others. Just as God has offered Himself as a sacrifice for us, we offer ourselves to God and to His people. *Agape* love is costly. Loving others will cost us something. It may mean that we give more money away to minister to the needs of others than we spend on ourselves and our own needs. It may mean a lunch hour spent in the hospital cradling and rocking a newborn child whose mother is unable to care for the baby's needs. It may mean an afternoon spent visiting a nursing home when we would really rather be playing golf. It may mean spending a vacation working on a mission team building a church in Honduras rather than surfing in Hawaii. It may mean praying with children in a classroom, or surrendering a prized seat to someone less able. *Agape* love is costly.

Agape love takes initiative. It is active. Love does not wait for an invitation or a free moment. Jesus Christ came into the world to die for our sins while we were still sinners. He did not wait until we asked for help. He did not procrastinate until it was a more convenient time for God! Love acts. Or as Jesus says, "Go and do …"

When John Wesley, the great English preacher and founder of the Methodist movement in England, was asked how the Christian should live, he responded, "*Do* all the good you can." Love *does*. Love acts. Love takes the initiative to benefit others. Love finds needs and ministers to them. Why? Because God sends us out into the world to be different. We are sharing His own *agape* love in all that we say and do!

A good question for all of us who are trying to live a life in the Spirit of God to ask ourselves is: How much love is evidenced in my life? At the end of this chapter, I will share with you ten ways that love can become a bigger part of your life.

We Are Being Made Perfect in Love

One last thing about Jesus. He not only said that we are called to love God with abandon: our whole heart, mind, soul, and strength. He also invited us to love our neighbors with joy. However, He raised the bar even higher. In Matthew 5:43-48, Jesus calls us to love our enemies. "Love your enemies and pray for those who persecute you, so that you may be children of your Father in heaven" (5:44-45 NRSV).

Why should we love our enemies? Because we want to be more like Jesus. God loves all people, even those who do not love Him in return. He still seeks them and extends His hand and heart to them even when

He is rejected. When we become Christians, God begins a new work in us. He begins to make us look more like His Son and less like the world. In the world, we all love our friends and people who love us, but few of us love our enemies or even pray for them.

However, when we begin to apply what Jesus teaches, we learn a remarkable lesson. When we pray for those who hate us or persecute us, our prayers not only begin to change our enemies, but we soon discover that our prayers begin to change us. The great miracle occurs as our own hearts change. We develop a greater capacity to love, even learning to love those who do not return our love.

As these changes come into our lives, we begin to become more like God, for God is love (1 John 4:16). When His love lives in us, it also is "perfected in us" (1 John 4:12). He perfects us as we grow in godliness. As we grow in love, we grow in holiness and begin to become the very people God intends us to be. His blueprint for our lives becomes a reality. "For this is the will of God, your holiness…" (1 Thessalonians 4:3). Over time, we become people of holy love—sharing ourselves, our resources, and the love of God itself with all of the world.

Jesus makes quite a claim here in Matthew, chapter 5: God is at work in us to make us more like Jesus. In fact, Jesus is so bold as to challenge us to "Be perfect, therefore, as your heavenly Father is perfect" (5:48 NRSV). God desires that our hearts resemble the heart of Jesus. He is pleased when our actions, even the loving of our enemies, look like the actions of His Son. Even more, He wants our *motives* to be like those of Jesus. Motives that are based in love. Motives that love God and love others.

Summary

Living in the love of God changes our lives! God's love—revealed to us in the life of Jesus and shared with us daily—transforms our views of the world, our actions, and our thoughts. We are changed by the remarkable love of God.

First, we realize that we are somebody. I am somebody. You are somebody. In God, I find my reason for living and a peace about dying. The love of God shows me who I am: I am His loved child, and He has made me for a special purpose. This is true of every one of us. God has a special plan for our lives. That plan becomes real when we learn to love Him and live in His love for us.

Second, we realize that everybody is somebody. Love is not just for me. God's love is for everyone. There is no one whom God does not love. Some of us may choose to reject that love, but that doesn't change it. The love of God may be rejectable, but it is not reversible. In the kingdom of God and in the eyes of God, everybody is somebody: the 81-year-old man struggling to remember who he is as his mind is ravaged by Alzheimer's; the 14-year-old girl winning the Olympic gold medal in gymnastics; the 18-year-old young man who leads the simple life of one with Down's Syndrome; and the 44-year-old woman profiting from the creation of her new software firm in Silicon Valley. God's love, and His sacrifice for us in Jesus, are available to all. God loves us first.

Knowing this means that we treat people differently. There is no one for whom Christ did not die. There is not one person who is not valuable to God. Loving God means learning to love others, even our enemies. That is the final lesson. We do not change people. That is God's work. He merely calls us to love and He will do the rest.

Jesus invites you to a life full of love. Enjoy!

Growing a Life of Love

1. Make a list of your enemies by name. Begin to pray daily for each name on the list. It may be easier to pray first for those with whom you have the best relationship, then move on to the ones who trouble you most.

2. Take some time one day a week to devote to serving in love another person who cannot possibly benefit you in return. Visit a resident at a nursing home, cuddle newborn children in need at the local hospital, or read mail for a blind friend.

3. Attend worship more than one time per week and seek to love God with your heart more fully. Perhaps attend worship in a setting or church that is different from your normal pattern. Worshiping with a person from another denomination may grow your capacity to love God in new ways.

4. Participate on a mission team with your church to serve persons in crisis. Help rebuild an area after flood damage. Help build a church in a new community or foreign country. Lead a vacation Bible school for children in a place where there is a need.

5. Begin to seek healing in a broken relationship. Take the first step toward patching things up with an estranged friend, an ex-spouse, or a hurtful colleague. Begin with prayer, then move forward into ways that can bring God's healing love—a letter offering apologies, a gift made in their honor, or perhaps a bouquet of flowers sent with no strings attached. Take the first step.

6. Keep a daily prayer journal to grow your capacity both to love God and to love others. Maintain a list of persons to pray for—both friends and enemies. Construct a daily list of three new blessings that you have received from God and give thanks to Him for those blessings. Use the journal daily as a means to deepen your prayer life in love.

7. Spend an entire day with your family and/or children. Uninterrupted. No distractions. No cell phones. No pagers. Hike, swim, picnic, read. Simply be together. Show them a personal sacrifice of your time. Have fun. Love one another with recklessness.

8. Give sacrificially. Anyone can give out of abundance. Make a gift to a scholarship fund, to a children's home, or to a hospice that is over and beyond your ordinary giving to God's ministries. Feel the pinch of doing without something so that others might benefit from your sacrifice. Give thanks to Jesus who sacrificed Himself for you without hesitation. Love God and others at the same time.

9. Send prayer cards to ten persons in prison. Offer to correspond regularly with one or more of these prisoners. Pray for their salvation and their healing. Pray for ways that you can help show them the love of God in a new way.

10. Spend a Saturday morning visiting a hospital rather than golfing, boating, reading, sleeping, or working. Visit the rooms of persons who have no visitors. Stay only briefly. Share a smile. Offer to pray. Show mercy. Love others as God has first loved you.

Joy

"...the fruit of the Spirit is love, joy, peace, patience, kindness, goodness, faithfulness, gentleness, self-control..."

GALATIANS 5:22—23a

Chapter II · Joy

"...the fruit of the Spirit is love, *joy...*"

Joy seems to be surprisingly scarce these days. As the pace of life quickens and the frenzy around us increases, joy is often the first thing to get squeezed out of our lives as joy finds it difficult to grow where stress is abundant. Perhaps stress is the weed that cuts off the growth of joy in our gardens, or perhaps the pessimism and negativism of the world serve as the killers of joy.

Scientists have even begun to prove that joy can be extinguished by negative people. In a recent study, researchers examined the habits and lives of unhealthy families. What they discovered may surprise you! Negative fathers and husbands breed negative spouses and wives. Moreover, negative parents breed sick, negative children. In other words, negativism is contagious. It is so contagious that our children can be swept up in its epidemic-like wave if we are not careful.

How many miserable people do you know? Do you notice how negative people always find and surround themselves with other negative people? When forced to interact with joyful people, do you notice how these people tend to persuade and discourage the more positive people around them? Negativism breeds more negativism. It is not difficult to find people to tell you why things won't work out like you hope and plan, and who love to rain on your parade. Most negative people are more than willing to share their dark thoughts and worries with you. In fact, they often can't wait for the opportunity!

These same researchers also discovered that, while negativism is highly contagious, joy is not so contagious. Joyful fathers do not necessarily foster joyful wives, nor do joyful parents always produce joyful children. Joy is not passed on as easily as negativism. Joy must be cultivated. Joy requires effort. Joy can be hard work.

However, the apostle Paul reminds us that joy is at the center of the Christian's life. We are a people of joy. Expressing the joy that God brings to our lives shows that we are Christians. From his prison cell—while in difficult circumstances that would cause most people, including most of us, to lose hope—Paul writes to the early Christians in the church at Philippi and instructs them, "*Rejoice* in the Lord always; again, I say, *Rejoice!*" (Philippians 4:4).

In fact, in a letter from prison to the Philippians, when we would expect to hear of Paul's burdens, sufferings, and worries, he mentions his "joy in Christ" more than twelve times in just four chapters. That is worth hearing: even in the most difficult times in our lives, we can rely upon a deep, abiding joy that comes from Jesus Christ. The world and our circumstances may press in and seek to crush us, but a relationship with Jesus will grow a joy in us that cannot be squelched.

Joy is at the very center of Christian life. Joy makes us different. Even when the world is closing in on us, we still have joy. Why? Three reasons: the simple joy of Jesus, the deep joy of living in Jesus, and the eternal joy of dying in Jesus.

The Joy of Jesus

Joy should not surprise us when we think about it. The angel told us to expect it. Remember? The shepherds were gathered out in the fields, minding their own business and tending to their flocks. It was an ordinary night . . . until the angel of the Lord stood before them, and the glory of the Lord shone around them. Can you imagine being at work one evening and having the glory of the Lord show up right in front of you. Wow!

Then the angel speaks: "Do not be afraid; for I bring you good news of great *joy* for all people" (Luke 2:10). Jesus, God's Son and our Savior, has been born. In Bethlehem. Great *joy!* For *all* people. The angel knew from the very beginning. Jesus' arrival in the world brings joy. So, too, does His arrival in our hearts and in our lives! With Jesus living within us, we have unspeakable joy, the very same joy that the angel shared with the shepherds on Christmas evening.

The wise men knew it, too. They traveled a great distance, following the star all the way from the East, not knowing where it would take them. They continued on to Bethlehem. "When they saw that the star had stopped, they were overwhelmed with *joy*" (Matthew 2:10). The wise men's search had ended. It ended in a stable in a little village that few people even knew about. It ended with their worship of the Christ Child in the manger. They were overwhelmed with *joy*.

Are you beginning to get the picture? *Jesus brings joy.* He brought joy when He was a newborn; He brings joy now to those who love Him. His joy is contagious. Christians have joy.

Jesus also taught us that to know God is to have abundant, unspeakable joy.

> The kingdom of heaven is like treasure hidden in a field, which someone found and hid. Then in his joy, he goes and sells all that he has and buys that field.
> MATTHEW 13:44 NRSV

The joy of discovering Jesus and the kingdom of God surpasses anything we will ever know. Consider the joy we feel when we find money on the sidewalk, or when we are out of town and unexpectedly run into someone we know, or when we have lost a piece of jewelry and then find it. It is amazing how much joy humans gain in finding and discovering something.

The joy of meeting Jesus for the first time, however, and gaining entry into the new way of life He offers exceeds the joy of everything else in life. There is no joy like that of being a part of the kingdom of God. Incomprehensible joy. Divine joy. Unswerving joy. That is Jesus Joy!

The Joy of Living in Jesus

The great joy Jesus brings to us when we first meet Him only serves to prepare us for the increasing joy that we experience in our new lives. We are kingdom people. We belong to God, and we are now free to live our lives the way He intended, free to please and serve our Lord. Free from the heavy weight of the demands of the world upon us. Free to be the people that God designed us to be from the very beginning.

This immense joy and freedom is made possible because of the empty tomb. Jesus put to death our sins once and for all. He gained victory over the forces of Satan and evil in the world when He died at Calvary.

But His death was not the end. No, it was only the beginning. Early in the morning, Mary Magdalene and the other Mary went to the tomb to see Jesus' body one more time. They hoped to anoint his body with oil, and then probably intended to pray and spend time with God as they grieved the death of their very special Friend. But when they arrived at the tomb, an earthquake shook the ground, and an angel appeared. Just as the angel did to the shepherds, he spoke to the two Marys.

> Do not be afraid; I know that you are looking for Jesus who was crucified. He is not here for He has been raised just as He said.
>
> MATTHEW 28:5-6

What do Mary and Mary do with this shocking news? How do they react to an earthquake and the arrival of an angel who shares with them that Jesus has been raised from the dead? They leave quickly with "fear and *great joy*" (Matthew 28:8). Mary and Mary were the very first to know that the resurrection was real. It was not just some bold prediction by Jesus. As they left the tomb and the angel that Easter morning, they ran squarely into Jesus Himself. Raised from the dead. No wonder they had *great joy!*

They had joy because they knew. They knew that Jesus was alive. They knew that God is bigger than life and bigger than death. They knew that death does not have the last word in our lives. They knew that Jesus was exactly who He said He was: the Son of God. He has prepared a place for us and He intends to take us to be with Him for eternity. He is the very Word of God made flesh and He proved to us that death is not the end. What unspeakable joy!

That joy changes how we live. We now live with the knowledge that God has a plan for us, and His plans extend even beyond the grave. We now see that we are spiritual people—more than natural, physical people, more than bodies or sophisticated animals. There is a whole world out there that we cannot see or touch with our hands. We no longer have to be confined by this world or its values. We are now a part of God's world. Oh, the joy!

Joy is just what Jesus intends for us. It is His goal that joy will be a vital part of our lives. Hear His words: "I have said these things to you so *that my joy may be in you and that your joy may be complete*" (John 15:11 NRSV). Jesus comes to bring us the joy of God. He introduces us to the Holy Spirit who completes us and makes us whole. Knowing God the Father, God the Son in Jesus, and God the Holy Spirit completes us with a divine joy—a joy like no other in the world. That is the fruit of the Spirit.

Possessing that joy helps us to endure whatever life may bring. The writer of Hebrews discusses how the early Christians faced sufferings, trials, abuse, persecution, the robbery of their possessions, and even imprisonment. How could they weather such storms? Because they knew that they "possessed something better and more lasting" (Hebrews 10:34)—salvation in Jesus Christ. This produces a joy in living that does not succumb to the world, a deep joy that cannot be extinguished by the hardships of the world or even by suffering. No, Jesus Joy is eternal and powerful.

We may not be able to see that spiritual world, but we belong to it now. Hear the words of Peter:

> Although you have not seen Him, you love Him. And even though you do not see Him now, you believe in Him and rejoice with an indescribable and glorious *joy,* for you are receiving the outcome of your faith, the salvation of your souls.
>
> 1 PETER 1:8-9

Knowing that glorious joy frees us to live joy-fully. We can thank those who criticize us. We can bless those who curse us. We can love those who hate us. Why? Because we have a joy that cannot be squelched or extinguished. That joy changes us. It changes the way we live. It changes us forever.

The Rev. Hosea Williams worked alongside Dr. Martin Luther King, Jr., during the Civil Rights movement in America in the 1960s. In fact, Williams was with Dr. King when King was assassinated in Memphis, Tennessee, by James Earl Ray. In a documentary, Williams describes how he felt when he saw Dr. King lying on the motel walkway, bleeding to death from the gunshot wound. "I wanted to go out and get a gun and kill the first white people I saw," he says. But he changed his mind "because Martin had taught me differently."

Even in times of violence and immense suffering, still that indescribable joy of Jesus allows us to live differently from the world. We see the world differently. We belong to God and to Jesus. We walk in the Spirit of God. Our values are different from the world's values. We can love and bless even when we are hated and cursed.

Oh, the joy! The joy of living in Jesus.

The Joy of Dying in Jesus

The parable of the talents in Matthew 25:14-30 is one of the greatest stories Jesus shared with us about how God wants us to live. A wealthy man, going on a journey, calls together his servants and entrusts his property to them. To one servant he gives five talents (a huge sum of money: about $2 million today), to another servant two talents, and to the third servant one talent. The first two servants invest the money in order to generate a return on investment for their master. The third servant, however, is afraid of losing the money he received. Rather than risking a loss, he digs a hole in the ground and buries the money.

When the master returns, he again calls his servants together to hear of their activity while he was away. The first two servants present themselves and the results of their work on his behalf. They have both doubled the sum of money that he entrusted to them. Hear how the master congratulates these two faithful servants:

Well done, good and faithful servant, you have been faithful
in a few things, I will put you in charge of many things.
Enter into the joy of your master!
Matthew 25:21,23

The third servant receives no such commendation. Instead, he receives a rebuke for his unwillingness to take risks or to work on behalf
of his master. Jesus calls him lazy, and the master casts him out of the
kingdom.

Jesus' point seems clear. God entrusts each of us with many things—
financial assets, as well as individual gifts and graces, not to mention
His immense joy. Moreover, He blesses us with the presence and the
power of the Holy Spirit. That is some kind of investment on His part.
He invests heavily in the heart and life of every believer and expects a
return on this investment. God calls us to work in and for His kingdom. He invites us to live our lives so that we share not only our gifts
but also His joy. He desires that our lives bear fruit just as He has grown
His fruit in us.

When we serve Him faithfully and bear fruit in our lives, God welcomes us into His eternal joy. Can you envision the joy of entering
heaven knowing that we have been faithful with our lives and faithful
to God's call to work for Him? *"Enter into the joy of your master."* I can
think of no other words I would rather hear now or in eternity. How
can you measure the joy of being a part of the kingdom of God? Of
living with God forever?

Anyone who has been in the room with someone who is dying knows
that there is a huge difference between those who die in Christ and
those who do not. When a person dies in Christ, there is a deep peace
and joy. Such persons move gently into the next life, calm with the
assurance of Jesus' promise of eternal joy. They find peace with their
families and peace with themselves. In death, such peace brings joy.

That is not always the case, however. Other persons die in turbulence, struggling and fighting with themselves, with family members,
and with God to the bitter end. Joy is strangely absent in these deaths.
Instead, there is just unrest.

There is joy in dying in Jesus. When we die, we know that He meets us and ushers us into His presence. Jesus has prepared a place for us after death. He has been raised, and so shall we. The joy that we experience now as we live in Christ is but the first fruit of the joy we will share then.

Oh, the joy of Christ. Christ in life. Christ in death. And Christ for eternity.

Growing a Life of Joy

1. Find a joy mentor. There is no better way to grow in joy than to be around persons who have it. Select a person in your life who has an abundant amount of joy. Spend time with him or her on a regular basis. This time helps to offset the effect that the negative people in your life may have on you. Let this joyful person teach you habits and routines from his or her own life that lead to increased joy in yours. Notice where they spend their time, what kind of things they do, and identify the sources of their joy. Learn to imitate those habits and routines.

2. Pick your friends and settings. Persons who participate in Alcoholics Anonymous know that one of the only ways to beat alcoholism is by changing their playgrounds and their playmates. An alcoholic simply cannot continue to hang around in the same places and with the same people as before. So, too, with joy. Actively seek to be in environments that cultivate your joy. Avoid settings and people who carp and criticize ceaselessly. Their negative outlooks will affect your own. Instead, surround yourself as often as possible with joyful people. Spend your time in places that encourage your own joyfulness. Remember the lesson that negative people breed negative people. Remove yourself as often as possible from the presence of such influences. This simple decision will have a dramatic impact on your life.

3. Remind yourself daily where your hope lies. "Whenever you face trials of any kind, consider it nothing but joy" (James 1:2). God knows you by name! He has a plan and a will for your life. He has sent Jesus to bring you home. Trust that promise of God. He will stand beside you. In fact, hear God's promise once more: "I will never leave you nor forsake you" (Joshua 1:5). When trials and sufferings come your way, remember that promise.

4. Let the joy of knowing and serving Jesus transform how you live. Develop a new level of trust in God that frees you to serve Him, even in the most difficult circumstances. For example, the churches of Macedonia were under intense affliction when the apostle Paul invited them to participate in an offering to benefit Jerusalem Christians in need. Rather than responding by wishing someone would help them, and criticizing Paul for having the nerve to ask them—the hurting—to help the needy, the Macedonians allowed "their abundant joy and their extreme poverty" to overflow in a wealth of generosity on their part. The joy of serving Jesus with our lives can overflow into an abundance of joy that helps us stand up to the worst circumstances. In other words, find your ministry and pursue it joyfully. Soon you will discover that the joy you find and receive in your service will fill the other parts of your life as well.

5. Endow your children with joy. Because negative, unhealthy behavior in families is contagious, Christians have a responsibility and an awesome task of passing on the joy of Christ to their own children. "I have no greater joy than this, to hear that my children are walking in the truth" (3 John 4). What brings your children joy? Playing with you? Reading together? Going to a movie with you? Do it! Introduce them to your own joy by praying with them, worshiping with them, and singing praises to God with them. Your children will learn joy by imitating you. Soon you will discover that your own joy will increase simply by absorbing some of your children's joy.

6. Make a thanksgiving list. Each day for a week in your quiet time, list specific things in your life for which you are thankful. Be specific. Name your joys one by one—for example, baseball, barbecue, bluegrass music, your pastor, a faithful friend or spouse, a colleague at work, and so on—and give thanks to God in prayer for them. As you pay more attention to these joys by listing them and thanking God for them, you will begin to no-

tice other things that give you joy. The more you notice, the more you will be able to cultivate the parts of your life that grow your joy.

7. Celebrate the Lord's Supper on a regular basis. Read the ritual from your church's worship service for communion. Some churches pray that God will use this time to "free us for joyful obedience" to Him. Remembering Jesus' sacrifice for us, re-enact the Last Supper and feel the presence of the Holy Spirit as you partake of the bread and juice. All of these lead to a deeper sense of joy in the Lord. Communion is Jesus' special gift to His followers. Use it. Celebrate it!

Peace

"...the fruit of the Spirit is love, joy, peace, patience, kindness, goodness, faithfulness, gentleness, self-control..."

GALATIANS 5:22—23a

Peace

"...the fruit of the Spirit is love, joy, *peace...*"

Peace. Pause for just a moment. Meditate on peace. Where do you need peace?

Where does the world need peace? In a church I attended, the pastor ended each service with a prayer for peace. Slowly and surely, we prayed each week for peace in the different areas of our lives. We prayed for peace in our hearts, in our homes, in our streets, in our relationships, in our cities, in our nation, and in our world. In a remarkable way, we all began to notice just how little peace existed in our world. Those prayers eventually began to grow peace in the lives of our church members and in the city where we lived.

Again, pause for just a moment. Meditate. Pray. Where do you need peace? Where does the world need peace?

There is no question that peace is God's business. Since we have been focusing on Galatians 5:22-23 for the fruit of the Spirit, it might be useful to look at the works of the flesh listed in Galatians 5:19-21. Before the apostle Paul shows us the fruit that God will bear in our lives when we walk with Him and live in His Spirit, he shows us the fleshly life. Fleshly, worldly living is the exact opposite of life in the Spirit.

Notice what he mentions as works of the flesh: "...sexual immorality, impurity, and debauchery; idolatry and witchcraft; *hatred, discord, jealousy, fits of rage, selfish ambition, dissensions, factions, and envy*; drunkenness, orgies, and things like these... those who do such things will not inherit the kingdom of God."

Of the fifteen works of the flesh listed, eight are clearly related to the lack of peace in our relationships with other people and other groups: hatred, discord, jealousy, fits of rage, selfish ambition, dissensions, factions, and envy. That is a big lack of peace, isn't it? Strife, discord, and anger in our relationships indicate a lack of peace that comes from the Spirit. Continual disharmony reflects an absence of peace in our hearts. When we live and walk in the Spirit of God, His peace will begin to saturate our lives, even our difficult relationships.

It is very clear that God cares about our relationships with other people. He desires for us to be in a right relationship with Him as well as our neighbors. When we live in the Spirit of God, we will soon discover peace sprouting up in our relationships. Anger and quarrels will fade, and peace will grow in their absence. Jesus leads to peace.

Those are important words to hear. They are life-giving words. Hear them again: Jesus leads to peace.

In homes where abuse and violence have taken root, Jesus leads to peace. In streets where gang members make the rules, Jesus leads to peace. In relationships, broken by gossip or deception, Jesus leads to peace. In lives fractured by addictions or failures, Jesus leads to peace. In nations, like England, whose rowdy, violent soccer fans triple the cost of security wherever they travel, or the United States, where the schools grow increasingly violent and dangerous, Jesus leads to peace.

Where there is turbulence and unrest, quiet and stillness are found only in the Lord Jesus. Life in the Spirit of God means peace.

Peace with God

Clearly, the first priority in our lives is to find peace with God. Without that, we will have no other peace. Achieving peace with God is the seed for growing the fruit of peace in the rest of our lives.

It is important to remember that peace is spiritual. It is not something that can be purchased or manufactured. It is not something we can do for ourselves. Peace comes from above; it comes from God. There is no other way.

It is a simple fact. God made humans to be in a relationship with Him. There is a part of us that is made for God alone, reserved for Him. He has a significant place in our lives. There is no substitute for His presence in our lives. When we choose not to acknowledge Him, our souls are restless. When we exclude God from His rightful place in our lives, our lives are incomplete. Without God, we are without peace. That is how we are made. The famous saint of the Church, Augustine, said it this way: "Our hearts are restless until they rest in you, O Lord."

The Bible plainly shows that peace is the work of Jesus. Just as the angel told the shepherds of a great joy in Bethlehem when Jesus was born, so too did the heavenly host sing to the shepherds of "*peace* on earth" (Luke 2:14). When Jesus rode on a donkey into the city of Jerusalem, as the people placed palms before Him, the crowds cried out to Him, "Blessed is the King who comes in the name of the Lord! *Peace* in heaven! Glory in the highest heaven!" (Luke 19:38). As He entered, Jesus wept for the city and said, "If you had only recognized the things that make for *peace!*" Jesus not only brings peace; He makes peace. When He was born, the angels proclaimed it. As He prepared to die, the people realized it. Indeed, as the angels proclaim, Jesus *is* peace.

That is why Paul refers to the gospel of Jesus as the "gospel of peace" (Ephesians 6:15). In fact, he invites us to put on the whole armor of God to protect ourselves from the world and from the devil. The world is a violent, turbulent place. Terrorists prey on the innocent and unsuspecting. Sin lures us away from righteousness. The devil seeks to lead us away from God and preys on our weaknesses. We need protection. With the armor of God, we can fend off attack and resist temptation. In that armor, the gospel of peace protects our feet.

Think about it for a moment. When we live in Jesus, we acquire peace. A peace from God. A divine peace. However, that peace not only lives in us, it protects us. When temptation comes and produces its turbulence and disturbance, the devil tries to swirl us around, confuse us, and disorient us. That has happened often in my own life, but let me share just one example. Time and time again, when I have decided to follow Jesus in a decision, the next thing to happen is a piercing temptation from the devil seeking to move me away from that decision. It always confuses me and makes me wonder if I am really listening to God. The devil sows evil with confusion and unrest. At those times, we can stand on the peace God has given us. This is important to know because temptation and the wiles of the devil will shake us and create a restlessness within us. That shaking can only be resisted with a deep spiritual peace. A divine peace.

Romans 8:1-6 captures this point best:

> There is therefore now no condemnation for those who are in Christ Jesus. For the law of the Spirit of life in Christ Jesus has set you free from the law of sin and death. For God has done what the Law, weakened by the flesh, could not do: by sending His own Son in the likeness of sinful flesh, and to deal with sin he condemned sin in the flesh, so that the just requirement of the law might be fulfilled in us, who walk not according to the flesh but according to the Spirit. For those who live according to the flesh set their minds on the things of the flesh but those who live according to the Spirit set their minds on the things of the Spirit. To set the mind on the flesh is death, *but to set the mind on the Spirit is life and peace.* (NRSV)

When our hearts and minds are set on the flesh and on the world, we have nothing but unrest and strife. Our hearts are unsettled, and our relationships are too. But, set on the Spirit and on the things of God, our hearts find peace and life itself.

Remember again the prayer of St. Augustine: "Our hearts are restless until they rest in you, O Lord." We are made for God. Without Him, we are restless and turbulent. Without Him, our souls and hearts will succumb to every temptation and every passion. We will be governed by our own whims and desires. We will love pleasure and live for the flesh. We will be unable to have peace with our neighbors and other people because we ourselves are without peace in our hearts. However, with God, we have a peace that can withstand anything. In fact, we have a peace "which surpasses all understanding and will guard your hearts and your minds in Christ Jesus" (Philippians 4:7) That occurs when the fruit of peace grows in our lives through the powerful presence of the Holy Spirit.

No one on earth can give us that kind of deep, spiritual peace. It can come only from our Maker. Before there is any other peace, we must first have peace with Him.

If you do not have peace with God, stop right now and pray. Ask God to still your heart and your mind. Pray with me:

> O Lord, how majestic is your name in all the earth. You created us out of nothing. You made me for your pleasure. Forgive me for living for myself. Thank you, Jesus, for forgiving my sins. Set me free to love you first in my life. Give me your peace. Come to me; live within me. Set me free, I pray. Amen.

Peace with Ourselves

Once we have obtained peace with God, we will begin to see the fruit of peace growing in our lives. Hear the words of Jesus:

> Peace I leave with you; my peace I give to you. I do not give to you as the world gives. Do not let your hearts be troubled, and do not let them be afraid.
> JOHN 14:27 NRSV

Where life in the world once brought fear, anxiety, and unrest, Jesus now brings a stillness and peace that we couldn't find in the world. Once we knew only troubles and fears, now we know the Master of the Universe, Creator of all. We have found our purpose and our direction. Jesus is our peace. He lives in us, and His Spirit guides us. We are free.

Peace with self means knowing who I am—a child of God. My value is not determined by the size of my savings account. I am not my job. I am not merely my father's son. I belong to Jesus. He guides my life. He prepares my way. I am at peace with myself.

Again, hear the words of Jesus:

> I have said this to you, so that in me you may have *peace*. In the world you face persecution. But take courage: I have conquered the world.
>
> JOHN 16:33 NRSV

Once we have peace within ourselves, the world and its powers no longer rule over us. Even persecution and suffering can be endured because our peace is not based on our health, or our rank, or our income. Our peace lives within us, and His name is Jesus. He is the living em*bodi*ment of peace within us.

Jesus has conquered the world. He invites us to follow Him to the same victory. We can now live the life God wants us to have. We are free from the demands of the world. We no longer have to please others first. We live to please God not man. We have peace. We know who we are. We now are "Jesus people."

The best picture of this peace comes in John 20:19-22. With Jesus gone, His disciples gather together in a house and lock the doors out of fear. They no longer have their leader, Jesus. They fear what the world might do to them. They fear for the future. What happened to God's Son? What will happen to their future? Where do they go now?

In the middle of their fear, Jesus suddenly stands before them in the middle of the room. What does He say? "Peace be with you."

The disciples are crippled by fear. Jesus says, "Peace."

His followers are bewildered and spiritually lost. Jesus says, "Peace."

After He shows them His hands and His side, with their nail holes from the cross, Jesus says again, "Peace be with you." Then He breathes on them and says, "Receive the Holy Spirit."

When His followers are lost, Jesus brings peace. When they feel alone, Jesus reminds them that He is there. He breathes on them and gives them the Holy Spirit.

Jesus has already breathed on you, believer. Feel His breath wash over you. Live in that knowledge and that power. Jesus offers His peace to you. Accept it. "Peace be with you." Live in peace.

Peace with God + Peace with Self = Peace with Others

Have you ever met someone who was always quarreling? Always fighting with others? Bickering, complaining, gossiping, criticizing? Think about it. That person has no peace. No peace within himself. No peace with her God. The evidence of that is this: they have no peace with others.

Until we have peace with God, we cannot have peace within ourselves. Until we have peace within ourselves, we cannot possibly hope to have peace with other people. I cannot have peace with others if I do not know who I am. That is why I use this simple equation to show the flow of peace in our lives:

Peace with God + Peace with Self = Peace with Others

Peace flows in that sequence.

First, we must find and receive peace with God. We do that when we acknowledge and accept the lordship of Jesus in our lives and begin to set our minds on the things of the Spirit. We then discover peace within. Remember, again, the words of St. Augustine: "Our hearts are restless until they rest in you, O Lord."

From the divine peace of Jesus, then, begins to blossom the peace of God at work in our lives. What does that look like? The Bible makes it plain for us:

> Bless those who persecute you; bless and do not curse them. Rejoice with those who rejoice, weep with those who weep. Live in harmony with one another; do not be haughty but associate with the lowly; do not claim to be wiser than you are. Do not repay anyone evil for evil, but take thought of what is noble in the sight of all. If it is possible, so far as it depends on you, *live peaceably with all.*
> ROMANS 12:14-18 NRSV

Walking in the Spirit and desiring the fruit of peace in our lives means that we live and act and behave peaceably. Revenge is removed from our motives and even from our vocabulary. Violence is rejected.

Jesus has made us new. We have different values from the world. Where the world is violent and vengeful, Christians sow peace. Fruit-full people spread peace wherever they go.

Fruit-full people are not concerned with looking good in front of others. They do not seek to impress nor to grandstand—attitudes that create unrest because they are false. We are who we are: Jesus people, Spirit people, God people. That is enough. Pride is replaced with humility. Evil is repaid with good. Violence is returned with peace.

How can this be? What would make a person not seek revenge? Why would anyone refuse to brag and impress? In a word, peace. Peace with God. Peace with self. Peace with others.

It is a divine gift. A fruit of the Spirit. Jesus breathes it. We live in it. The peace which surpasses all understanding.

Growing a Life of Peace

1. Know His peace. Take time three times each day to pause and remember the words of Jesus, "My peace I give you." Feel His breath wash over you as He breathes His peace and His Spirit on you. Bask in the warmth of His power and live in peace.

2. Develop a "Psalm habit." The book of Psalms is full of every human emotion imaginable: fear, joy, sadness, confidence, despair, elation, and many others. The psalms speak the very things we all wish that we could say to God. By reading one psalm, or spending time in the same psalm every day for a week, the peace of God can grow within our souls. Read the psalms, pray the psalms, study and meditate on the psalms, live in the psalms for a while. Allow them to breathe the peace-filled word of God into your soul.

3. Pray for peace. Continue to cultivate your prayer life. This will have a direct impact on your level of peace with God and peace with yourself. In turn, your prayer life will affect your peace with others. Covenant with God to pray daily. Your prayer life probably will benefit the growth of peace in your life more than any other fruit of the Spirit. Use a prayer journal to record the things, areas, and persons in your life that prevent peace. The co-worker who constantly annoys and nags. The fear of the future and its uncertainty. The worries over health issues. The list goes on and on. Pray that God will teach you to trust in Him for all things. Prayer leads to peace.

4. Pray for your enemies. Write down their names one by one. Take time to pray for each enemy individually by name. Pray for those who hurt you or persecute you. Pray specifically that God will help you to return evil with good. Pray that God will take away the spirit of revenge and bitterness that is within you. Praying for your enemies may not change them; however, it will change you. Peace begins in your prayers. To multiply the ef-

fects of this kind of prayer, encourage your children to do it as well. Help them to see the value of praying for enemies and thinking about how we respond to those who hurt us.

5. Confess your sins. Spend time each week in confession and self-evaluation before God. Be honest with Him and with yourself. Examine your heart for the areas that need His cleansing touch and share those with Him. Invite God into every area of your life and mind and heart. Remove those things within you that prevent peace.

6. Become an agent of peace. Write a letter of apology to someone you have hurt, even if he is a despicable person or she is a gossip. Share your heart so that God's peace might flow in you and through you.

7. Focus on the positive and accentuate it in others. Contribute to greater peace in your relationships by remaining positive even when others are supremely negative. They may not encourage peace, but you can.

8. Pray for peace in our world. Write down the nations and regions where there is conflict (use a newspaper or magazine as a source). Pray for those areas, perhaps spending one week on each region. For example, pray this week for Ireland and Northern Ireland. Next week, pray for Bosnia. The following week, pray for the unrest in American inner cities such as South-Central Los Angeles.

9. Memorize Romans 12:14-18. Recite the passage when you awaken in the morning. Recite it as you drive to work. Recite it silently when controversies and conflicts arise in your day. Recite it with your children or spouse to ensure that it becomes a central part of your home. This will help you learn to live peaceably. Peace will become an internalized part of your life and spirit.

10. Fast when you pray. Make it a part of your spiritual life. If you have medical concerns, you may first need to consult a doctor. Begin small—fast for one meal. Grow into the ability to fast for 24 hours or more, always drinking liquids to avoid dehydration. Fasting helps to reveal the things that control us. Food is one of those things, but fasting also helps reveal our anger and our lack of peace. What is the reason for your unrest? What is blocking your ability to have peace in your heart and in your relationships? Fast when you pray. Pray that God will reveal the sources of your own lack of peace and set you free to have peace with Him and peace with others in your life.

Patience

"...the fruit of the Spirit is love, joy, peace, patience, kindness, goodness, faithfulness, gentleness, self-control..."

<small>GALATIANS 5:22—23a</small>

Patience

"...the fruit of the Spirit is love, joy, peace, patience..."

Patience is a virtue. Unfortunately, it is not a virtue that comes to me naturally! Even more unfortunately, that is true for many of us, isn't it?

However, God assures us that patience is a fruit of His Spirit. It grows within us as the Holy Spirit works on our hearts. God is patient, and He desires to help us grow in patience.

Incidents in my own life routinely remind me of my own shortcomings in patience. I am a classic Type-A personality, naturally impatient and always wanting to get on to the next task on my to-do list. I am not proud of this trait, but I am growing to recognize that patience will be a struggle for a person with my DNA. Sitting in traffic recently with a friend of mine, after having waited twenty minutes in line to purchase tickets to a movie to be shown four hours later (because all the other earlier scheduled showings were already sold out), we politely stopped short of a traffic light at the exit of the theater's parking lot. We hoped to allow cars to pass in front of us and cross through to the other side of the parking lot.

We waited patiently, proud of the Spirit's work in us, as cars passed in front of us. The driver of each car seemed grateful for the break in the logjam which had been preventing their progress. This plan worked well for us, but evidently it was not so pleasing for the occupants of the car behind us. After a minute or two, they quickly swerved out of line and darted in front of us in the line at the light and thereby cut off the crossover traffic, and all other cars, in the parking lot altogether. Of course, they had a Christian symbol fish sticker on the rear of their car! A moment earlier, I had been proud of my level of patience, but with this intrusion of the new car in our path, my patience went out the window and instead was quickly replaced with "road rage." I felt like my entire world was being attacked. This act seemed egregious to me. Not a pretty scene.

The fruit of the Spirit is patience. Hear the words of Scripture. God is patient, and He desires to grow patience in you as well. As a child in a worship service said, "Patience means you have to wait a lot."

The Bible has a lot to say about patience. In fact, it describes for us three kinds of patience which I call: end-time patience, social patience, and personal patience (or endurance).

End-time Patience

As believers, we wait for the Lord. That is a simple but important fact. We wait for the coming of the Lord. We wait for the completion of His plans in our world. We wait for the arrival of the kingdom of God. We wait for our souls to be united with Jesus forever. We wait for justice to be brought upon the evils and trials of this world. We wait for the ultimate fulfillment of the Lord's promises to His people. We wait. That is end-time patience, all Christians living with an eye toward God's eternal future.

Of course, God works on His own time with His own ways. We, as humans, can merely wait and anticipate what He will do. It is comforting to know that He is already at work in the world and in our lives right here and right now. But there is also a sense within each of our spirits that God is up to much more in the world than at first meets the human eye. His ways are often mysterious, and we can only wait to discern what He is up to.

God is at work carefully bringing about His kingdom, working to bring all creation unto Himself. The Holy Spirit's work in each believer's heart is certainly a part of that greater work of God, but God is about the cosmic business of completing creation and bringing all that He has made to consummation. What a blessing that day will be when Jesus arrives for His children! When God ushers in His kingdom once and for all! When evildoers are swept away and impurity is banished from the world! When we are restored to our eternal place near the throne of God to be joined with believers from all times and all places in singing the praises of our Lord and our God! What a day! Come, Lord Jesus, come.

Patience for that day is end-time patience. We Christians know the outcome of history. We know where we are headed. We already know the ending. We have the assurance of God's final victory. In the meantime, we wait. End-time patience.

God wins in the end. That is good news. That's the single focus of the book of Revelation. Because we know the ending and we know our eternal destination, we can live differently than the world lives. We can have a patience that the world does not possess. We know that the ways and purposes of God will prevail in the end. Therefore, we can live our lives according to His principles for our citizenship is in heaven (Philippians 3:20). We need not worry that we will not get enough things or fulfillment in this lifetime. We do not invest ourselves completely in the achievements of this worldly life for we know that there is a life to come that is more important and more rewarding. Life with God is eternal; it has no end. Knowing that fact makes patience much easier to grasp and to possess. We do not lose heart when things do not work out as we hope right now for we know there is coming a day when the purposes of God will prevail. Right will be made right, and evil will be no more. Christians know that that is worth waiting for..

That is kingdom patience—knowing that God wins in the end. Knowing that we do not have to frantically go through this life trying to get all the goods and all the pleasure that we can. Instead, we are free to lead patient lives, serving God, and anticipating the completion of His work in the world. We possess a patience that the world does not have. End-time patience.

Hebrews 6:9-12 expresses end-time patience this way:

> Even though we speak in this way, beloved, we are confident of better things in your case, things that belong to salvation. For God is not unjust; He will not overlook your work and that love that you showed for His sake in serving the saints as you still do. And we want each one of you to show the same diligence so as to realize the full assurance of hope to the very end, so that you may not become sluggish but imitators of *those who through faith and patience inherit the promises.* (NRSV)

This end-time patience grows in us as we grow in the Spirit. We labor now, knowing that God will reward our labors in the end. Some rewards will come in the here and now; others will come later in the kingdom. Nevertheless, God always rewards faithfulness and, because we know this, the Spirit can work patience in us. Our hearts can be put at rest when the rewards are not apparent right here and right now. Why? Because we know that God is faithful and will stand by us in the end. That is worth working for, and that is worth waiting for.

That kind of patience is beyond value, isn't it? The Holy Spirit provides a whole level of internal peace that allows us to live richer, fuller lives. We can afford to be patient because we know that this life is not the end but merely an anticipation of eternity with our Lord. We know that there is more to this life than meets the eye. And best of all, we know the Maker. He holds the future, and He holds the answers. We merely wait on Him.

End-time patience. When the Holy Spirit begins to bring His fruit into our lives, this end-time patience is one of the first things to appear. That is true because end-time patience begins to blossom at our conversion, at that time when we finally realize that God is eternal and that He offers eternity to us. An eternal focus brings end-time patience. Because we know God, we have something worth waiting for.

Social Patience

The second dimension of patience that the Holy Spirit begins to work in each believer's heart is what I call social patience. Patience with the other people in your life. Social patience blossoms directly out of end-time patience. As we learn to have a kingdom view of the world and of our lives, the Spirit then is able to move us to a deeper level of patience with other people. In other words, the more we know God and trust in His eternal ways and victory, the more we are able to be patient with the other people around us. We learn that we are still growing in the Lord and that others are too. Best of all, we know who holds the future.

The apostle Paul teaches us that God expects and desires this kind of patience in us.

> As God's chosen ones, holy and beloved, *clothe yourselves* with compassion, kindness, humility, meekness, and *patience. Bear with one another,* and if anyone has a complaint against another, forgive each other; just as the Lord has forgiven you, so you also must forgive.
> COLOSSIANS 3:12-13 NRSV

Patience originates in the Holy Spirit of God. And patience means learning to be patient with other people, even to the point of forgiveness. God says, "Clothe yourselves with … patience. Bear with one another…" In other words, just as God is patient with me and my failures, so, too, does He desire that I will be patient with my neighbor, my child, my co-worker in our struggles together. Bearing with one another even when our shortcomings and failures are apparent. That is social patience.

The Bible usually links these three ideas: patience, bearing with one another, and forgiveness. For example, just as he does in Colossians, Paul says in Ephesians 4:1-2: "I, therefore, the prisoner in the Lord, beg you to lead a life worthy of the calling to which you have been called, with all humility and gentleness, *with patience, bearing with one another in love.*" So it seems natural, then, to take a look at how the Spirit will bring out patience and forgiveness in you as you walk in the Spirit.

Studying the life of Peter is a good place to start. Think of Jesus' relationship with this disciple. In this one relationship alone, Jesus demonstrates how the three concepts of patience, bearing with one another in love, and forgiveness are all linked together.

1) Jesus calls Peter to leave his fishing business and "follow" Him to become a fisher of men. Peter obeys Jesus immediately. (Mark 1:16-20)

2) Peter is a physical witness as his own mother-in-law is healed by Jesus. (Mark 1:29-31)

3) Peter witnesses firsthand the remarkable life of Jesus as He heals the sick, feeds the multitudes, teaches the crowds, and rebukes the Pharisees. Jesus routinely invests significant amounts of time and energy in Peter.

4) Peter confesses that Jesus is the Messiah when Jesus asks "Who do you say that I am?" Peter clearly has been paying attention and knows who Jesus is. (Mark 8:27-30)

5) In spite of the fact that Peter knows who Jesus is, he nevertheless rebukes Jesus for teaching the disciples that the Son of Man must die and rise again. *Hear that: Peter rebukes Jesus Himself.* Maybe Peter doesn't get it as much as we thought he did. In turn, Jesus rebukes Peter with the famous words, "Get thee behind me, Satan, for you have your mind set not on the things of God but on the things of men." (Mark 8:31-33)

6) Peter then witnesses Jesus' transfiguration on the mountain when Elijah and Moses appear. (Mark 9:2-8)

7) Peter is present when Jesus enters Jerusalem, cleanses the temple, and instructs His followers about the coming crucifixion and the end times. He shares in the Lord's Supper in the upper room when Jesus eats with his disciples for the last time. (Mark 14:12-25)

8) Jesus tells Peter that he will be the one disciple to deny Him. Peter rejects that word. Jesus is patient with him even as Peter falls asleep in the Garden of Gethsemane while Jesus prepares to die. (Mark 14:26-42)

9) Peter denies Jesus not once but three times (Mark 14:66-72) and is nowhere to be found as Jesus dies, is buried, and is raised. (Mark 15:33–16:8)

What is the point of all this? Very simple: Peter ebbs and flows. He shows signs of greatness as he leads the disciples. He shows remarkable weakness as he fails Jesus and even denies Him. He shows great insight by knowing and understanding who Jesus is. He shows a huge gap in understanding by telling Jesus that the Son of Man should not suffer and die. Yet Jesus stands by Peter. He does not give up on him or cast him out of His group of followers. Jesus is patient with Peter. Peter ebbs and flows. Jesus does not. Jesus is constant; He is patient. Always. Even to the end. Because His Father is patient.

Even when Jesus knows that Peter will deny Him, still He takes Peter along to the Garden of Gethsemane. Still He is patient with Peter. Even to the end. And when Peter breaks down and seemingly is lost after denying Jesus three times, the risen Jesus returns to make a special appearance to him. Their conversation went something like this:

Jesus: "Simon, son of John, do you love me more than these?"
Peter: "Yes, Lord, you know that I love you."
Jesus: "Tend my sheep."

Jesus: "Simon, son of John, do you love me?"
Peter: "Yes, Lord, you know that I love you."
Jesus: "Tend my sheep."

Jesus: "Simon, son of John, do you love me more than these?"
Peter: "Yes, Lord, you know everything. You know that I love you."
Jesus: "Feed my sheep." (John 21:15ff)

In the very end, Jesus is patient with Peter and restores him to the leadership role among the followers. Jesus is patient time and again with Peter. Even when Peter has seemingly dropped the ball in the worst way, Jesus still has the last word. And that word is forgiveness. That word is restoration. That word is patience. When Peter falters or stumbles, still Jesus is there. When Peter rebukes or denies Jesus, still Jesus bears with Him in love. And in the end, Jesus forgives Peter. Patience, bearing with one another in love, and forgiveness. Social patience. Patience with others. God shows us what that looks like in Jesus. And God desires to grow that same kind of patience in each of us. Amazing, isn't it?

In the same way that Jesus stood by Peter and loved him even in the face of denial and failure, the Spirit of God brings forth fruit in us even when we fail Him. Even as we learn to bear with one another in difficult circumstances. Even as we learn to forgive one another when we don't want to do so. This may be a hard lesson for you, but it is still true. God wants to grow His patience in you. His Spirit will do just that. God is patient. Always.

Being patient with those who hurt you, with the boss who overlooks you, with the parent who does not recognize your achievement and love, and with the neighbor who shuns you, are not natural human things to do. Bearing with people who mistreat you and showing patience with difficult people are not natural human responses. They are the work of the Spirit alone. You cannot do these things without the Spirit of God in your life. However, with the Spirit, you cannot help but grow more patient and forgiving with all of these persons in your life. It will happen. Why? Because God is patient. The very same remarkable patience that God showed with Peter, He will share with you.

If you are growing in the Spirit, then you will be growing in forgiveness and in bearing with others in love. There is no way around it. If your life is cooperating with the Holy Spirit, you will grow in patience. Remember, the Spirit grows all of His fruit in the heart of each believer. Patience will be part of your blessing from God. You may not be perfect at patience. But you will be growing in it. It is not optional. God does it! It is not of your own power. It is a gift of God's grace. You will be more patient and forgiving of the failures and shortcomings of others this year than you were last year. And next year will show more signs of growth in your forgiveness and social patience than this year has. And the year after that will be more fruitful than next year. That is the work of the Spirit. That is social patience.

Personal Endurance and Patience

The work of the Spirit brings a patience that goes even deeper than the end-time patience, which tells us that God wins in the end. And His work brings a patience larger even than the patience we have with the other people in our lives. The work of the Spirit bears fruit as we learn to be patient and endure through personal suffering. The Spirit makes Himself known to us as we learn to experience the hand of God *in* our suffering rather than *in spite of* our suffering. This lesson may be the hardest one to hear and the hardest one to learn, but it is also the most fruitful. God can and does grow our patience by using the suffering in our lives to draw us closer to Him and to form us in His image. He does not cause suffering, but He can use it to grow us.

Achieving this level of fruit is a sign of maturity in your life as a Christian. When you can endure personal suffering and still look God in the eye with a heart of thanksgiving and joy, that is personal endurance and patience worked only by the Holy Spirit. When you can look at the agonizing death of Jesus on Calvary's cross and see God's salvation, that is a life-changing experience. It is a remarkable thing to live in the knowledge that God can and does work for His good in all things. Again, the letters of Paul give us great wisdom. Hear these simple words. Say them aloud.

> Rejoice always.
> Pray without ceasing.
> Give thanks in all circumstances; for this is the will of God
> in Christ Jesus for you.
> 1 THESSALONIANS 5:16-18 NRSV

The hardest part of this personal patience is the fact that it almost always comes through suffering. I do not know why. I do not invite it. I certainly do not encourage it in my own life. Yet, for some reason, time and again, the hand of God uses the worst times in my own life to grow my spirit and to bring about more fruit. The deepest lessons often have come through the University of Life and Hard Knocks. Some things simply cannot be learned in a book. We will learn them only when we live them.

God is good. I know that to be true in all things. And I learned that to be the case in the worst three years of my life. Anita, my wife, and I have lived fairly easy lives to be honest, but for three years we endured intense personal suffering in a way we hope never to replicate. At the same time, that period of suffering strengthened our faith lives more than anything else either of us has ever experienced. Through that suffering, we learned patience, we deepened our own love for each other, and we learned about the heart of a God who walks alongside us in the valley of the shadow of death.

For three years, while I was in graduate school, we lived more than a thousand miles away from our families at a time when our two daughters were in their infant and pre-school years. We expected that distance to bring some challenges, but we never expected to learn the faith lessons that we did. During those years, my body was afflicted with an intense, chronic, acute case of ulcerative colitis. A case that we and our doctors were never able to get under control, not even with experimental treatments. A case that caused me to spend several hours each day in the bathroom, writhing in pain, while watching my body wither down to thirty pounds less than my optimum weight. A case that began to affect the lives and outlook of our young daughters and ultimately resulted in my having my entire colon removed and replaced by a bag that I still wear on my body. At the same time, Anita suffered two miscarriages. In fact, there was one day when both of us lay in the same hospital, doors apart, undergoing medical procedures while a caring relative took care of our girls. That day was made worse a few months later when another doctor diagnosed me with an early case of melanoma, the skin cancer that kills.

Remarkably, somehow, through this period of being isolated from family while enduring a crucible of physical suffering (keeping in mind that our experience pales in comparison to the lives of some others I have known), we each experienced the hand of God in new and vital ways. Through the love and assurance of friends in our new town, through the prayers of other believers scattered around the globe, and through the presence of the Holy Spirit in the darkest hours, somehow I grew closer to God.

Even more remarkably, God worked to rearrange my priorities and help me to see what is truly of value in this lifetime. A number of things that I had previously hoped to do in my life and my ministry all of a sudden fell by the wayside. I realized that God had clearly given me the mission of sharing His gospel of good news about Jesus and that many of the other things in my life were a distraction. Because I no longer knew for sure how long I might live, God made it quite clear to me that it was time to get on with the task He had given me. In the face of death, I learned a healthy impatience for the things of life that simply don't matter. More importantly, I learned to be patient when things look dark or bleak. I learned that God is still in control, and I can trust Him. In other words, I learned a deep, abiding patience because I had nowhere else to go but to God. Doctors could not help, my education could not help, my ambitions and goals could not help. Only God could be my help and my hope. He taught me that patience. Without suffering, I would never have learned that.

It is true for me. It is true for you. It was true for the apostle Paul. How else do you explain these verses written from prison?

> Yet whatever gains I had, these I have come to regard as loss because of Christ. More than that, I regard everything as loss because of the surpassing value of knowing Christ Jesus my Lord. For His sake I have suffered the loss of all things, and I regard them as rubbish, in order that I may gain Christ. . . .

> I want to know Christ and the power of His resurrection and the sharing of His sufferings by becoming like Him in His death.
> PHILIPPIANS 3:7-8,10 NRSV

How else would Paul have the ability to exhibit patience and peace with great personal suffering other than by the work of the Spirit? Remember, he is in prison as he writes this, nearly unable to fulfill the mission that God has given him and withering alone in a prison cell. Yet he is prospering in Christ! He is filled with the joy of knowing Jesus better through His suffering for the gospel's sake. I know no one on earth who could exhibit such patience in these circumstances by any means other than the Holy Spirit. And the Spirit was able to bear this personal patience and endurance in Paul's soul through tremendous sufferings that go far beyond imprisonment.

In 2 Corinthians, chapters 6 and 11, Paul reminds the Corinthians of his afflictions, hardships, calamities, floggings, lashings, beatings, stonings, shipwreck, robberies, and starvations on behalf of the Church and his personal mission for Jesus. Yet, somehow Paul comes out of these events loving God more and desiring Jesus more fully. He endures the worst of life and emerges even more passionate about his mission. That is Spirit work.

It will be true for you, too. When we walk in the Spirit, the Spirit turns the worst parts of our lives into opportunities for bearing fruit. More often than not, the fruit that is borne is patience. We learn to trust God in all things and to live by Him and through Him, rather than on our own timetables and schedules. God is patient, and He desires to grow that patience in our lives and souls.

And it is that patience that allows the believer not only to hear but truly to understand and believe that indeed "…all things work together for good for those who love God, who are called according to His purpose" (Romans 8:28). Indeed all things do work together for good because God is good. As our patience grows, that simple fact of God's goodness grows. That is the work of the Spirit. The Holy Spirit of God. The Spirit who brings personal endurance and patience.

The Holy Spirit did that same work in the prophets who endured suffering to speak truth in the name of the Lord. James 5:10-11 teaches us that those who endure are called "blessed." There is no better example of the blessings that come from endurance than Jeremiah who endured and was faithful even in the face of failure and rejection.

Faithfulness to God can sometimes bring no results. We do not like to hear that, but it is true. Jeremiah worked for years to speak God's truth. When Judah faced destruction by the Babylonians, Jeremiah preached the message of repentance, calling the Jews to fall down on their knees before God, but Judah failed to listen. They rejected Jeremiah completely.

We like results. We like to see the fruits of our labors. None of us like to work hard and see nothing come from that work. Yet sometimes, our hardest work for God yields nothing. We stand up for truth, we work hard, and still the powers of evil seem to prevail. God still calls us to be faithful. Personal patience and endurance.

Faithfulness to God can bring hostility. The more Jeremiah preached, the more hostility he endured. Yet he remained faithful—so faithful that he continued to preach throughout his life even in the face of greater and more violent opposition. He endured imprisonment, exile, and death threats. He endured attacks. And still he remained faithful to God's Word and truth.

We do not like to be attacked. We go out of our way to avoid conflict. We prefer the comfort of popularity and choose the path of least resistance. Yet, the call of God can and does lead to rejection and even attack. It is that kind of personal endurance and patience that God seeks to work in you and in me. In fact, it seems clear that the closer we get to the heart of God, the more the world will attack us. And the more we are attacked, the closer God draws us to Him. And in that drawing near, God shapes us to be more patient, trusting in Him alone for the future and in Him alone for the victory. We can be patient for we stand with God.

In the end, the Spirit draws us close to God. The farther we walk with God, the more we learn to stay the course and trust Him to provide for us. The more we grow in the Spirit, the more patience we have for we slowly grow to learn that God is in control. We do not know everything now, but we shall later. Trust in God, allow end-time patience to saturate your life, let God lead you to greater levels of personal endurance and patience. That is God's heart. God is patient, and He will grow patience in you. The fruit of the Spirit is patience.

Growing a Life of Patience

1. Cultivate and memorize simple prayers to use during stressful times. When life is crazy around you, the kids are screaming, the phone is ringing, the traffic isn't moving, the enemies are attacking, call those simple prayers to mind and allow God's Spirit to saturate your life. Memorize prayers like: "Come, Lord Jesus, come" or "I love you, Lord" or "We know that all things work together for good for those who love God and are called according to His purpose" (Romans 8:28).

2. Take slow deep breaths as a way to inhale the Spirit of God. When stress builds and impatience grows, remind yourself of the patient presence of God by taking slow deep breaths that fill your body and enlarge your heart and soul. Breathe in the Spirit of God and allow it to permeate your body and soul. Feel the Spirit move through you, bringing hope and new life. Patience will grow.

3. Don't sweat the small stuff. As a boy years ago, I heard a great preacher share that basic message. Now it is a best-selling book. However, we can never learn to let go of the small stuff that overtakes us without God in our lives. Better yet, as my boyhood preacher taught me, "It's all small stuff." End-time patience teaches us that God holds the details of the world in His hands and is at work for a much larger purpose. Everything else is just details. Remind yourself to let it go.

4. Look for God and His work in unexpected ways and unexpected places. God really is at work doing a great thing in the world and in your life. Let go of some of the details and begin to look for how and what God is up to. For example, a number of years ago, our church's music minister announced that he was leaving the ministry. He and I were close friends. Our families shared much time together. The church loved how he led worship, and we had no idea how we would ever replace him. We were devas-

tated. Two days later, my phone rang. Another friend of mine who lived halfway across the country shared with me that his wife had accepted a new position in our town and that they would soon be moving nearby. He was beginning the process of looking for a job. I knew well his work in the music field and his competency for leading worship. Two days prior, we had been without hope. Now we had a capable replacement to lead our worship. God does provide if only we let Him. Pay attention. Look for what He is doing.

5. Embrace failure. Stumbling and falling can become a means to grow personally and even learn to accept the failures of others. I hate to fail; you hate to fail. We don't like others to see us fail or fall short. However, if we are growing and stretching for God, we will fail—often. If we are not failing at something, we are not trying. Accept that and use it to grow. When you come to terms with your own failures and shortcomings, you will soon find yourself being more patient with other people around you who fall short. Accept your own imperfections, learn to accept those of others, and soon patience will blossom in your own life. My failures are too numerous to mention. However, one in particular from my years as a pastor stands out in my memory. A number of years ago, I launched a Thursday night service with a new style of worship. We hoped to reach people who found the idea of traditional church unappealing. We thought that having a service on Thursday instead of on Sunday would show folks that we were serious about being different. We promoted, advertised, and worked hard to share the news of our new worship experience. It worked—for about two weeks. A large crowd showed up the first Thursday night. The crowd shrank a bit the following week, and within six months, only about twenty people attended on a typical Thursday evening. People just didn't think about going to church on a Thursday. We failed to succeed in what we had hoped to do. However, we

tried. We tried something new that we believed God wanted us to do. There was the victory. We loved and trusted Him enough to do something to reach new people, even if it did not work.

6. Make a forgiveness list. Pray daily for those who have hurt you or let you down. This will grow your patience more than anything else you can do. Pray first for those for whom it is easiest to pray. Over time, God will shape your heart to allow you to pray for those who have wounded you and hurt you the most deeply. As you continue to pray, God's Spirit will move in you to grow patience. Patience with others.

Kindness

"...the fruit of the Spirit is love, joy, peace, patience, kindness, goodness,
faithfulness, gentleness, self-control..."

Galatians 5:22—23a

Kindness

"...the fruit of the Spirit is love, joy, peace, patience, *kindness*..."

Jesus warned us in the Gospel of Mark about loving ourselves most of all. A scribe asked Him, "Which commandment is the most important one of all?" His answer? "Love God .... and *love your neighbor as yourself*" (Mark 12:28-31).

"Love your neighbor as yourself." Why do we have such a hard time with this? The world all around us is full of evidence that we find it tough to love other people at all. Even kindness seems to be in short supply.

In fact, at its worst, the world is violent and harsh. Teachers now have to be trained to protect themselves against attacks from their students. Fathers assault referees at youth ballgames. Overflowing prisons burst at the seams because we cannot control the violence in our streets. Grotesque violence fills the productions of our movie theaters and television sets. For much of the world, unkindness is just a way of life.

But unkindness is not just "out there" in the world. More often, unkindness shows itself in very simple, everyday ways. We make rude hand gestures and mutter obscenities to one another while we wait in traffic. We hurry to nose our cart in front to be next in line at the grocery store. We gossip about our co-workers at the coffee machine.

Why do we treat other people as if they don't matter? The answer is shockingly simple: we love ourselves more than we love anyone else. We are still not quite sure that other people are as important as we are. That is the sin of pride: when we love ourselves more than others.

Ironically, in times of war, the veil of unkindness often comes off and is replaced by unity. When our nation goes through a crisis, like the one experienced on September 11, 2001, we refocus our hearts and attention on things that "really matter." And then, suddenly, we become kind to one another. Isn't that odd? In good times, we find it difficult to be kind, while in times of war and strife, kindness becomes commonplace.

Why is that? It is very simple: when we focus on the things that "really matter," we realize that human beings, human life, the people around us, *are* what "really matter." All the other things that once seemed so pressing become less important, and we take stock for a moment of the other people in our lives. Then we show kindness. In other words, when we really value life and seek to love other people, kindness becomes a priority. When we are kind, we show that we value other people as much as we value ourselves. "They" are just as important as "we" are. Kindness flows out of recognizing the simple truth that people matter. All kinds of people. We were all made by the same God. We all matter to Him. God's people know that, and their lives show it.

That is exactly what the Bible teaches us about kindness.

What Kindness Is: Ephesians 2:7

God is kind. The evidence is all around us.

Ephesians 2:7 teaches us that God shows us "the immeasurable riches of His grace in *kindness* toward us in Christ Jesus." God is kind, and Jesus is the living proof of that kindness. Jesus shows us what God's kindness looks like in living form. Though we may be unkind to other people, or even to God Himself, He still takes the first step and gives us the unmistakably kind gift of Jesus.

There are four key parts to this important Biblical statement:

Immeasurable riches

When God saw the world struggling, wandering off on its own, lost in its own ways and devices, He sent His Son. He offered Jesus to the world then, and He offers Him to you and me now. When we are lost, God sends Jesus to find us. When we turn our backs on God, He calls us home with the kind gift of Jesus. Jesus: God's own Son, offered as a gift to the world. That is "immeasurable riches."

Jesus is grace beyond compare: a God who offers His Son to the entire world, even to you and to me. That is divine kindness. Kindness even when we ourselves turn away or are unkind to God. Who can possibly put a value on that? Christians are "immeasurably rich."

Kindness

Webster's Dictionary defines "kind" as the quality of being good-hearted. Kindness is like love, goodness, and gentleness in its actions, but it is more of a state than an act. Kindness, or having a good heart, lives itself out in loving, good, gentle ways and acts. Very simply, more than anything else, kindness is a "heart condition."

We know God's heart. We have seen His heart in Jesus. Because God is kind, He shows us His heart in the goodness, love, and gentleness of Jesus.

Toward us

God values every one of us. He values each life He creates. And His heart desire is that we will value one another, too. Remember, again, Jesus' greatest commandment: "Love God... *and* love your neighbor as yourself." Love other people as much as you love you. Jesus' message has kindness at its core: "See other lives as just as important as your own and treat people that way."

Jesus shared that supreme divine kindness with every life. Think about the people with whom He spent most of His time: children, lepers, sick women, men possessed by demons, tax collectors, prostitutes, and sinners. Hardly a list of the rich, famous, and powerful! No, Jesus spent the bulk of His time with a ragtag, motley crew of oddballs and misfits. He even welcomed the wealthy and the important, but on His terms not theirs. Jesus shows us the kind heart of God as He welcomes the smallest and loves even the most sinful among us as we seek God.

His message was so very simple, but it is still hard for us to comprehend: Every single human being, every life created by God, matters to Him. No one is more important or significant or valued than any other. Here's the catch: If each person matters to God, each one should matter to us. That God-centered "heart condition" alone produces kindness.

In Christ Jesus

Hear it once more: Jesus *is* God's kindness. God's big gift of kindness came in a small package of swaddling clothes, a baby sent to save us. God is so kind that He even became flesh (John 1:14).

Jesus represents the kindness of a God who became one of us. He came to us so that we could come to Him. God's loving gift of Jesus to you and to me is a miraculous act of kindness that sets the tone for our lives.

In fact, that is what Jesus does. He shows us God. He is the Word of God made flesh, living right here among us. The fact that God decided to become one of us tells us that He values us. He did not come as some kind of alien or foreign being. He came first as a fetus in Mary's womb, then as a baby born in a manger, then as a child, and then as a man. Jesus is God's supreme gift of kindness to us. He embodies the kindness of God. He is God's living kindness.

God sent Jesus to seek and to save us. Like the woman looking for a coin she has lost, or the shepherd looking for *one* sheep who has strayed from the flock, so too does a kind God search for each one of us (Luke 15). He desires us, seeks us, loves us, even when we turn away. He sends Jesus to bring us home. The seeking presence of Jesus is God's supreme act of kindness. That is what Jesus does. He expresses God's kindness toward us by searching for us, claiming us, and showing us the ways of His Father. That is what we were made for: to live with Jesus in the ways of God.

In the end, God's kindness is intended to change us. "Do you not know that God's *kindness* is meant to lead you to repentance?" (Romans 2:4).

1) God is kind toward us because He loves us.

2) God is kind to us because He hopes that we will repent of our unkindness toward Him. He yearns for us to love Him as He loves us. God is kind to us even when we are unkind to Him.

3) God is kind to us because He hopes that His kindness will change us to be kind not only to Him but also to one another. God wants to change us into the persons He designed us to be.

When you and I stray, God is still there, kindly offering Jesus to you and to me. That is kindness. Divine kindness. Kindness is Jesus. Kindness is a fruit of God's Spirit, and that fruit tastes sweet.

What kindness is not: 1 Peter 2:1-3

Ephesians teaches us about the kindness of Jesus, God's living kindness. In 1 Peter, we learn what kindness is not.

> So put away all malice and all guile and insincerity and envy and all slander. Like newborn babes, long for the pure spiritual milk, that by it you may grow up to salvation; *for you have tasted the kindness of the Lord.*
> 1 PETER 2:1-3

We taste the fruit of God's kindness when we love Jesus. He touches our hearts with the kindness of God, a God who loves us before we even know who He is. A God who loves us and desires us even when we are remarkably unkind ourselves. Jesus touches us and makes us whole. His kindness is overwhelming and unlike anything else in this world. He is kind because His Father is kind. And God wants that same kindness to take root in your life and mine.

What does that kindness look like?

God's fruit-full people will:

1) "Put away malice."

"Malice" is the intent to injure. God does not seek to injure people. God's Spirit does not seek ways to harm others. Thus, God's people should put away the desire to hurt others, and instead begin to grow in kindness. When the world piles on to make fun of the last child picked to be on a team, kindness will instead offer encouragement and grace. Kindness will seek to help, not hurt.

It's true on playgrounds; it's even true in divorces. I recently saw a bumper sticker that read, "I still miss my ex-wife, but my aim is improving." Evidently, this man still has a little malice that needs to be put away!

The fruit of the Spirit is kindness. God's kindness is encouraging; it builds up others, not hurts them.

2) "Put away guile."

"Guile" is the act of deceiving. God does not deceive. He is open and straightforward. However, we humans often deal in deception. We deceive when we negotiate unscrupulously in business. We deceive when we do not reveal our behaviors and misdeeds to our spouses. We deceive when we fail to tell the whole truth. While the world will say, "*Caveat emptor:* let the buyer beware," kindness will deal openly and truthfully.

When my wife and I bought our first house, we were quickly initiated into the mysteries of real estate: commissions, inspections, termites, flood plains, and surveys. We learned a lot about disclosures, too.

On the disclosure sheet, the seller of the house comments on each area of the house he is selling (foundation, roof, plumbing, etc.) and is supposed to disclose any past problems or current issues affecting that part of the house. In our case, the seller made comments in each area but left blank the section regarding the roof. We soon learned in our inspection that the roof had numerous leaks causing lots of damage which the seller simply "forgot" to disclose.

The fruit of the Spirit is kindness. God's kindness is straightforward and truthful, upright and true. His people will be, too.

3) "Put away insincerity."

"Insincerity" is being dishonest or not genuine. We are insincere when we give false praise or when we fail to tell things accurately. We are insincere when we make others believe things about us that simply are not true or when we pretend to like someone whom we deeply resent and distrust. While the world offers false praise and flattery to someone important in hopes of personal gain and recognition, kindness remains humbly quiet, resting on the values of God rather than the values of the world.

The fruit of the Spirit is kindness. God's kindness is sincere, genuine, and true. His people will be, too.

4) "Put away envy."

"Envy" is selfishly grudging what another person enjoys. Envy resents others who have more than we do or are more fortunate than we are. Envy bears grudges against those who win when we do not. Envy secretly hates those who are good at the things we are not good at. Envy eats at the heart from the inside out. Envy is destructive.

Jeff and Bob had similar dreams. Both wanted to go to the same prestigious law school. When Bob was admitted but Jeff was not, Jeff's heart ached so badly that he ended the friendship and moved away. His envy was simply too much for him to bear, and he dragged that burden behind him for years. While the world grudges, kindness rejoices in the successes and achievements of others. While the world resents the beautiful new home of a brother, kindness offers to celebrate a house-warming to share in the joy. Clearly, kindness is not manmade; it is possible only through God's heart-changing Spirit.

The fruit of the Spirit is kindness. God's kindness rejoices in the good fortune and success and happiness and comfort of others.

5) "Put away slander."

"Slander" is injuring someone by false report. Slander is when I try to make myself look good by making others look bad. Slander disregards the truth and desires to hurt. Slander willingly and gladly destroys another person's good character and good name. Ironically, slander also destroys the character and good name of the slanderer, too.

While the world drags the name of enemies through the mud and the media, kindness looks for the high road, remaining silent in the face of slander rather than injuring another for no cause. While the world spreads misinformation about competitors, kindness seeks to compete in an open and fair way.

The fruit of the Spirit is kindness. God's kindness is commending, looking for the good and praising it.

∽∾∾

You have tasted the kindness of the Lord. That is a remarkable thing. God has forgiven you when you were dishonest. He has overlooked your envy of others and has not held your insincere tongue against you. Instead of crushing you, He has been kind to you. He has given you Jesus, and with Jesus comes change. A change of heart, a change of ways, a change of life. Experience life in God's kindness.

Jesus brings the kindness of God into your heart. As that kindness takes root in your life, kindness will flow from your heart. It can be no other way; kindness is a fruit of God's Spirit. A consistently unkind person is not living in Jesus or walking in the Spirit of God. How do we know? Because God is kind. And His people are, too.

Kindness Lived Out in Word and Action: Joshua 2

When Moses died, Joshua took over the reins of leadership for Israel. He was nervous. He had never led before. Moses had always been in charge. And now they were about to enter the Promised Land. What a challenge Joshua faced!

The Israelites were nervous, too. They were at the most important point in their history, and now they had a new leader. With Moses, they knew what to expect, but now Joshua was at the helm, and it was time to cross the Jordan River into the land of Canaan. All God's promises were coming to pass, but first they had to trust Joshua to take them there.

Joshua was scared. The Israelites were scared. And the Promised Land lay just ahead.

What was the first thing Joshua did? Pray.

What was the second? He appointed two spies to go into the city of Jericho to see what lay ahead. The spies secretly entered the city and spent the night at the house of a prostitute named Rahab.

When the king of Jericho got word of two foreign spies being in his city, he sent word to Rahab to turn them over to him. However, Rahab knew that these spies were on God's side and represented His work in the world and in her life. She understood that she had a simple choice: to stand with God or against Him. She chose the latter, even if it cost her enormously.

Thus, Rahab protected the spies from the king's soldiers, hiding them in her home, helping them to escape from Jericho safely, and then preventing the king from finding out about their plan. She risked her own life, extended hospitality to the two Israelites, and stood firmly with God. Why? She said, "The Lord your God is indeed God in heaven above and on earth below" (Joshua 2:11). Rahab knew exactly what she was doing. She was turning from her ugly past to a bright new future with God.

Rahab showed kindness to God by showing kindness to His people. She specifically mentions that she has dealt "kindly" with the Israelites and hopes that they in turn will deal "kindly" with her (Joshua 2:12). And indeed they do. When Jericho is taken over by the people of Israel, Rahab and her family are made a part of the people of God (Joshua 6:5). Rahab becomes a part of God's people. Her kindness reflects the kindness of God. In fact, later, in Matthew 1:5, she is even mentioned as an ancestor of Jesus! A foreign Canaanite woman, earning her living as a prostitute, sides with God, acts in kindness, and becomes a part of God's own people. Then Jesus is borne from her line. A remarkable story. Kindness.

What does this story of Rahab teach us about kindness? First, kindness is active not passive. God is not a passive, do-nothing God. The Holy Spirit changes us, and those changes make us act differently. Faith is not a spectator sport. Kindness acts, it is proactive and takes the initiative. We stand on God's side.

Second, kindness takes risks for God, even in the face of opposition, hostility, and danger. Kindness recognizes God's work and seeks to be a part of it. Kindness takes God's people in, shows them hospitality, and protects them from that which would harm them. In other words, kindness often swims upstream against the world. Rahab was willing to be kind to God's people because she hoped that God would, in turn, be kind to her. She recognized the work of God and chose to become a part of it, even when she had to put her own life on the line. Kindness is courageous. The world is often harsh and violent, so it takes courage to be kind. Where the world might criticize Christians as being door-mats, softies, or pushovers, Christians know that kindness requires the greatest strength of all: to stand with God. Kindness comes from the heart of God.

However, the New Testament makes kindness even more clear. We do not have to earn God's kindness as Rahab tried to do. Instead, God is already kind toward us. Remember? God offers Jesus Christ to us. Our kindness to other people merely reflects the kindness that God has already shown us in Jesus. Our kindness is genuine and true because we love and serve a God who has been eternally kind to us. We can face hostility, even violence, and return it with kindness because our trust and hope are in a God whose ways are kind. We stand with Him.

We have tasted the kindness of the Lord. The Holy Spirit frees us to be courageously kind. The fruit of the Spirit is kindness.

Growing a Life of Kindness

1. Think before you speak. Your grandmother was right. If you cannot say something kind, say nothing at all. That's not as easy as it sounds, though, is it? That requires thinking before I speak. It requires thinking before I act rather than merely acting on impulse or emotion. "Will my words harm anyone? Will my actions injure?" Too often, we act before we think. We should start making a conscious effort to think first, act second. Remember how Joshua prayed before he did anything. Kindness puts away malice and guile. Kindness is truthful, and it tries to build up rather than injure.

2. Listen, really listen. Spend time with a child. Actually spend time with him. Put away the cell phone and the calendar. Turn off the television or the car radio. Listen. Listen carefully. Listen well. Show kindness by demonstrating to a child that she matters. There is no more valuable gift or expression of kindness than to really listen.

3. Practice "random acts of kindness." These acts can be remarkably powerful. The recent movement with that name had a point. Pay someone's bill at a restaurant or their toll on a highway. Pick up the trash in a neighbor's yard. Wash your teenager's car. Share a kind word with the cashier at the grocery store. Assist a mother with children—or anyone—by holding a door open. Look for small ways at various times throughout the day to share a small sample of God's kindness and grace with a complete stranger or a good friend. Acts of kindness benefit both the giver and the receiver.

4. Start each day in prayer. Ask God to help you see the world as your place to minister rather than as a place to fear. This is God's world, and you are God's child. Like Rahab, you can be an agent of kindness. See the people around you as persons in need of God's kindness and grace rather than as mere objects in

your life. Listen to the friend whose father has just died; share a meal with the neighbor just diagnosed with cancer; assist the family struggling to stay afloat after a job layoff; notice the children at school who don't get invited or included. In other words, offer kindness to the same people whom Jesus noticed and valued. Then you will be living in the Holy Spirit.

5. Try to live one day without telling any lies. Notice how hard it is to be truthful and kind! Notice the remarkable level of attention, energy, and restraint that it takes. We are used to fudging, cutting corners, and offering empty flattery or white lies. Honesty may mean sharing difficult news. Kindness may mean choosing to say nothing at all. God is straightforward and true.

6. Set aside a full day each month to do nothing but demonstrate God's divine kindness. Visit a nursing home with flowers or a children's home with toys. Help those who cannot possibly help you or repay you. Help them in the name of the One who has shown God's kindness toward you: Jesus. Offer them the same grace and kindness that Jesus has offered you. Their lives matter to God, and so does yours.

Goodness

"...the fruit of the Spirit is love, joy, peace, patience, kindness, goodness, faithfulness, gentleness, self-control..."

GALATIANS 5:22—23a

Goodness

"...the fruit of the Spirit is love, joy, peace, patience, kindness, *goodness...*"

God is good. All the time.

How true it is. God *is* good.

Good is the opposite of evil. Good is the force that created the universe. God looked at His creation and saw that it was "very good" (Genesis 1:31). Creation is good because God is good.

If God is good, then it makes sense that goodness would be a fruit of His Spirit. God made us in His image, so we have the ability to be good. But, at the same time, we sin, we turn away from God, we serve other gods or ourselves, and we fail to honor God. The Bible describes sin as "missing the mark." God has a plan for us, but when we fail to obey Him, we "miss the mark" for our lives. That is what sin is: rather than seeking to be good and to do good, we often fall short of God's hopes and dreams for us.

Even when we try to do God's will, there frequently is something inside of us that leads us astray. Romans 7:15 describes that inner struggle when Paul writes, "I do not understand my own actions. For I do not do what I want, but I do the very thing I hate." Goodness is hard, isn't it? We want to be be good, but on our own, we simply cannot achieve goodness.

We fall short, and that is where Jesus comes in. When we talk about goodness, Jesus is a good place to start.

Merciful Goodness

> Surely goodness and mercy shall follow me all the days of my life, and I shall dwell in the house of the Lord forever.
> PSALM 23:6 NIV

In most of the books of the Bible, goodness is closely linked to mercy. In fact, Jesus uses mercy to teach us about goodness in three ways.

1. *God's Merciful Goodness Toward Us*

We are sinners. We fall short of the glory of God. We want to please God and serve Him, but somehow, we get sidetracked. God invites us to a life full of joy, peace, and love, but instead we often find ourselves living a life full of anger, greed, and envy. God is holy, and He has holy hopes for our lives. But we take God's beautiful creation of life and twist it, distort it, abuse it, and disregard it. God wants us to have life, but often, because of our sinfulness, we choose death. By the measure of God's holiness and our sinfulness, we surely deserve to die for our disobedience.

So what does God do about it? Does He destroy us? Does He sentence us to death? No, He makes a new covenant, and covenants are marvelous things. Covenants are better than contracts. Covenants last. Covenants don't break. God makes a new covenant with us in Jesus, and He keeps His promises. Because God is good. All the time.

Remember the words of Romans. The apostle Paul describes God's miraculous and merciful covenant with us. A covenant that God makes because He is good. He shows us that merciful goodness by (1) sending Jesus in spite of the fact that we didn't ask for help nor did we deserve it, and by (2) allowing Jesus to die in our place for our sins.

We were sinners, and God loved us anyway. Jesus is simply a free gift of God's merciful goodness. A gift of forgiveness, a gift of salvation. God is good, and Jesus proves it.

> But God proves His love for us in that while we were still sinners Christ died for us.
> ROMANS 5:8 NRSV

And the news gets better. Because God is good, He not only forgives us for sinfully wasting His creation of life, but He also stands on our side from the moment we believe in Jesus. He takes us in. God makes us His own. He forgives us, restores us, and begins to make us new. He stands with us. God is mercifully good.

> If God is for us, who can be against us? He who did not withhold His own Son but gave Him up for all of us, will He not with Him also give us everything else?
> ROMANS 8:31-32

Again, the news gets even better. God's merciful covenant cannot be broken. His love cannot be destroyed or removed from us. It lasts forever, and it supercedes all things. The new covenant is a sure and certain promise of God. God is good. Always.

> For I am convinced that neither death nor life, neither angels nor principalities, neither things present nor things to come, neither power nor height nor depth, nor anything else in all creation will be able to separate us from the love of God in Christ Jesus our Lord.
> ROMANS 8:38-39

Think about what God has done. He has made an unbreakable covenant with you and me. His promise is sure: Receive the gift of Jesus, be forgiven and be made new. We didn't deserve it. We didn't earn it. We didn't even ask for it. God simply gives it. All we do is receive.

That proves God's goodness. We deserve to die, and instead God gives us forgiveness and new life. We deserve wrath, and instead God is merciful. God is good. All the time. In all places. Always.

2. *Our Merciful Goodness in Forgiveness*

Once we receive God's gift of new life and forgiveness in Jesus, God begins to teach us how to forgive. He begins to make us good just as He is good. He works in us to help us live up to the fact that we were made in His own image. He injects His goodness into us. And it begins with forgiveness. If goodness is the fruit of God's Spirit, then forgiveness is the branch on which goodness grows. A good heart forgives.

Unfortunately, we humans are not very good at forgiveness. We are good at holding grudges. We are good at holding other people to perfect standards that we cannot possibly meet ourselves. We are good at letting hurts fester inside of us. We are good at being perfectionists who criticize anyone at any opportunity.

We don't understand mercy very well. We like it when others show mercy and forgiveness to us. But we find it challenging to show mercy and forgiveness to the people around us. A sign in Baltimore, located on the wall outside of a church and convent, read: "Trespassers will be prosecuted to the fullest extent of the law—Sisters of Mercy." Evidently, even the Sisters of Mercy struggle with mercy, too! Probably a good move legally but it is kind of difficult to put "prosecute" fully and "mercy" in the same sentence, isn't it? Humans have a hard time with merciful goodness.

But God's way is a different way. God forgives and He desires to show us how.

Jesus makes it clear: Forgiveness lies at the heart of being a Christian. That makes sense, of course, because forgiveness lies at the very heart of God.

> But I say to you that if you are angry with a brother, you will be liable to judgment; and if you insult a brother, you will be liable to the council; and if you say 'You fool' you will be liable to the hell of fire. So when you are offering your gift at the altar, if you remember that your brother has something against you, leave your gift there before the altar and go; first be reconciled to your brother. Then come offer your gift.
> MATTHEW 5:22-24

God has given us the model: *Forgive first.* He did it for us in Jesus. Now He invites us to do the same with our brothers and sisters. And He invites us to be generous with our forgiveness. Not to withhold it in some stingy container brought out on special occasions but to be a sprinkler of forgiveness, liberally distributing it around our lives like water on parched grass.

> Then Peter came and said to Jesus, "Lord, if my brother sins against me, how often should I forgive? As many as seven times?" Jesus said to Him, "Not seven times, but, I tell you, seventy times seven."
>
> MATTHEW 18:21-22

Unlimited forgiveness! Bountiful mercy! God is good. He is miraculously merciful and generous. His forgiveness proves it. And He desires to give us forgiving hearts and generous spirits to make us good. After all, we are made in His image!

3. *Our Merciful Goodness in Compassion*

God's goodness teaches us to be merciful not only in forgiveness but also in how we see the world. Through His eyes, we view the world with compassion, as a place in need of His healing mercy and goodness. We notice those who are hurting and those who are broken. God's goodness invites us to be attentive to the least, the last, and the lost among us. The Holy Spirit gives us new eyes to see.

The Bible reminds us of this over and over again. Nearly every one of the prophets from Isaiah and Jeremiah to Micah and Nahum spends enormous amounts of energy calling the Israelites to care for orphans and widows, the dying and the weak, and the elderly and the newborn. God's people share God's goodness with all.

Zechariah put it this way:

> Thus says the Lord of hosts: "Render true judgments, show kindness and mercy to one another; do not oppress the *widow, the orphan, the alien, or the poor;* and do not devise evil in your hearts against one another." But they refused to listen and turned a stubborn shoulder.
>
> ZECHARIAH 7:9-11 NRSV

Even when we are not interested, God is very interested in how we treat those who are forgotten or lost. We may care only about ourselves, but God calls us outside of ourselves to a life of goodness. Goodness. Mercy. Forgiveness. Generosity. Compassion. These are God words.

God has taught me this lesson so many times that I have lost count. I tend not to allow God's Spirit to help me see the world as He sees it. For example, when I attended seminary, my first-year internship placed me as a chaplain at a homeless shelter for families with children. The shelter was located in an Episcopal church in the suburbs. As part of my placement, I spent an evening each week, dining and talking with the residents. I listened to their stories and lives. I heard their hurts and often prayed with families who had lost jobs or homes. Each week, my fellow students and I met with the pastors who led this church and reflected on what we were learning about God, about life, and about people.

Early in my time there, I shared that I felt outraged that this church would try to help some of these families whom I felt were clearly trying to take advantage of the goodness of this church. Their stories did not add up, they seemed to be angling to get as much from the church as they could, and I thought they should have to prove that they deserved everything they got. The lead pastor of the church, very gently and kindly, turned to me and said, "I would rather be called a 'sucker' than be called 'cold-hearted.'"

Lesson learned yet again by one Mr. Allen Hunt: God calls us to be generous and good, merciful and forgiving, even to those who might take advantage—*especially* to those who might take advantage. We do not need to "have the advantage." God alone is sufficient. God is enough. We are not called to be right all the time. We are called to be forgiving and good. Because God is forgiving and good, and He wants to make our hearts like His.

God's forgiveness is not limited. Nor is His goodness and mercy. He invites us to be the same.

Generous Goodness

God's goodness is also expressed in His generosity. He is good, and He is a giver. In fact, all that we have and enjoy in this lifetime has God as its source. Think about David's prayer when the people of Israel had given abundantly and generously to build God's temple. David prayed and blessed the Lord in the presence of the assembly:

> David said, "Blessed are you, O Lord, the God of our ances- tor Israel, forever and ever. Yours, O Lord, are the greatness, the power, the glory, the victory, and the majesty; for all that is in the heavens and on the earth is yours; yours is the King- dom, O Lord, and you are exalted as head above all. *Riches and honor come from you, and you rule over all.* In your hand are power and might; and it is in your hand to make great and to give strength to all. And now, our God, we give thanks to you and praise your glorious name. But who am I, and what is my people, that we should be able to make this free- will offering? *For all things come from you, and of your own we have given you."*
>
> 1 CHRONICLES 29:10-14 NRSV

God's goodness expresses itself in everything that we have and in all the world around us. God is the Supreme Giver, the Source of all. We belong to Him. He is the Giver of Life. When we grow in God's good- ness, we will grow in giving as well.

Giving is joy. To give is to become more like God who delights in our giving and even multiplies it to bless others. "God loves a cheerful giver. And God is able to provide you with every blessing in abundance so that... you may share abundantly in every good work" (2 Corinthians 9:7-8).

Sadly, few of us are givers. We hoard our resources, use them on ourselves, and fail to see that God is the Source of all blessings and all things. We like to see our things as "our" things. When we do so we become self-absorbed creatures who live in the flesh rather than in God's Spirit. Ugly.

Not so much physically ugly (although greedy eyes and stingy faces are not very becoming) but just not very enjoyable to be around. Misguided hearts are ugly to behold.

When we are envious—when we want what others have—that isn't a very pretty trait, is it? Someone who always resents other people; someone who spends time dwelling on what they don't have. None of us grows up wanting to be that way, but many of us find ourselves living "ugly" lives.

For example, I once saw a list of the 200 wealthiest people in the high-tech field. On it were the names of folks who have accumulated the most wealth in the computer-related field. As I read, I saw his name— a fellow I used to work with. In fact, we started with the same firm on the same day. I later left to go into the ministry, and a few years later he left to start his own software firm. He is now worth $220,000,000. I am now worth about $14.63!

To be honest, for a moment, I read that list and looked on with envy. Sadly, that says more about me than it does him. Ugly, isn't it?

For a moment, the competitive side of me wanted to earn and get and acquire as much as I could as quickly as I could. My eyes became green with envy. If I had to say what I think the ugliest human trait is, I would have to say it is greed.

Maybe that is why I find greediness so unappealing because I have struggled with it enough in my own life. It is a temptation for me to want everything just for me—to hold on to money—to become a scrimping, hoarding, conserving, penurious, stingy, parsimonious miser.

And I can tell you where that leads: to a cold heart, a jaundiced eye, a suspicious nature, and to a lonely life with very little love. When greed sets in, goodness is forced out. The two cannot co-exist. We either live in the flesh, or we live in the Spirit. And goodness is a fruit of God's Spirit.

Marge Schott knows something about that. She spent all her life acquiring wealth and hanging on to every penny she could. She owned the Cincinnati Reds although she was later forced out of that role by popular demand. The players despised her. Her staff loathed her. In fact one employee, quoted in *Sports Illustrated*, said, "She is the single worst person I have ever known. Spiteful, mean-spirited, and evil." And another staffperson said, "She is the most calculating, cold person I've ever known." There was not much goodness in her heart. In Christmas of 1998, she told the staff there was no money for holiday bonuses and then threw bags of candy on each of their desks. Bags of leftover candy from a children's promotion donated by the Leaf Manufacturing Company. Printed on the back side of the package: "Win a trip to the 1991 Grammys!" (Reilly, Rick. Heaven Help Marge Scholt. *Sports Illustrated.* May20,1996)

Now, the opposite of greed is generosity. And you know what generosity looks like: One who shares—gladly, willingly, and with joy.

I think of Robbie Ray whom I read about in *Interpreter* magazine. The writer described how every day for the past thirteen years the 77-year-old woman gets up at 2:00 a.m. to bake cakes—her own special-recipe cream cheese pound cakes. She bakes three to eight cakes per day which she ships to customers all over the country. The ingredients cost her $4 per cake and she sells them for $10 each, donating the proceeds (100 percent, not just 10 percent) to the youth ministry fund at her church in New Albany, Mississippi. In thirteen years, she has baked over 7,000 cakes and raised more than $70,000 to touch the lives of students with the gospel of Jesus Christ. Her goodness overflows. Her generosity proves it every day.

As far as I know, she is still going strong. In fact, she says, "My goal is $100,000. After all, baking keeps me going." Clearly she understands what Winston Churchill meant when he said, "We make a living by what we get; we make a life by what we give." Generosity is a good indicator of goodness.

Why does Robbie Ray do it? Why does she rise early every day simply to give the fruits of her labor away?

It could be for a lot of reasons. One of my friends in ministry suggested a few:

- Do you think it is because we are commanded to give? The Bible teaches us that over and over again.
- Do you think it is because she likes to watch God take what she gives and then multiply it to touch lives of countless others—as Jesus did with the fishes and loaves when He fed the 5,000?

- ✍ Do you think it is because she feels called to sacrifice? Maybe she knows there is no real love or honor without sacrifice.

- ✍ Do you think it is because she feels like it is the very least that she can do, given how she has seen others called to give their entire lives for Jesus in mission?

- ✍ Do you think it is because she knows that she is a co-worker with God, laboring in His vineyard and being a blessing to others? Perhaps she envisions herself standing next to missionaries and Mother Teresa and Martin Luther King, Jr., as she stands baking in her kitchen each morning.

- ✍ Do you think it is because she is a channel of grace and knows that she will therefore be blessed more fully?

- ✍ Do you think it is because she wants to give thanks to God for all that He has done? To give back an expression of her gratitude to God as did the one leper out of ten who returned to give thanks to Jesus.

- ✍ Do you think it is because she wants to overcome the temptation to be idolatrous in her own life? Maybe she knows full well that acquiring and getting just leads us to worship what we acquire and get. Our stuff often owns us more than we own it. Robbie may be seeking to overcome that temptation to admire her stuff.

- ✍ Do you think it is because she wants to overcome the temptation to withhold any part of herself from God? Perhaps Robbie understands best of all what it means to be completely given over to God.

- ✍ Do you think it is because she wants to grow in the image of God—a God who is first and foremost a Giver, a God who gives us His Son and gives us eternity?

It is only my opinion, but I think that Robbie Ray sees her baking as a way of abandoning herself fully to God in order to love Him with all her heart. She knows that her generosity allows her to bear the fruit of goodness. The fruit of God's Spirit.

God has called her to serve Him, and she is doing her best to live a life worthy of that calling. As a believer, there is no other way.

I see Robbie Ray serving in goodness just as the woman in Mark 14 who anointed Jesus' feet with expensive oil, weeping and caressing them with her hair. All the while, those around her wondered why she would invest that extravagant oil on Him. She abandoned herself fully and completely to loving the Lord. Her generosity expressed the goodness growing fruitfully in her heart.

Goodness is a fruit of God's Spirit. And our generosity merely expresses that goodness, the goodness of a giving God overflowing in us.

Growing a Life of Goodness

1. Learn to give. Learn to share your financial resources:

   ∾ For God's mission through tithing. If you have never tried tithing (giving 10 percent of your income to God's mission), try it for one month. Watch how God uses your measure of goodness in remarkable ways to grow His fruit in you.

   ∾ To help persons in need around you. Do you have a sibling whose family is struggling? Do you have a neighbor who has lost a job? Do you work with a custodian or laborer at work who can barely provide for his own family? Find the people in your life who are experiencing need and try to find ways to ease that need.

   ∾ By sacrificing some of the abundance you enjoy in your own life in order to advance God's kingdom in the world. Give up something from your life (an expensive hobby or habit, a valued possession, a regular dining-out experience, etc.) and give the money instead to God as an expression of your love for Him. Abandon yourself to loving God fully just as the woman did in Mark 14.

2. Have mercy on someone you know whose life has been broken. Help a young unwed mother get training for job skills, assist a friend who has been downsized by praying and walking alongside him during the time of joblessness, provide means for housing to a woman who is fleeing an abusive husband. Be an instrument of God's mercy.

3. Stand in unity with Christians in other countries who do not enjoy the same abundance, comforts, and freedoms that you do. Pray for the house churches in Cuba; give to a group that assists the persecuted, indigenous church in Vietnam; find a way to assist the ministers and leaders of the underground church movement who are presently in prison in China. Express your gratitude to God for His blessings in your life by specifically

remembering these Christians who worship at the risk of losing their lives. Allow your generous goodness to bear fruit in the lives of your persecuted brothers and sisters.

4. Forgive someone who has wronged you and experience merciful goodness in real life. Perhaps someone is indebted to you financially, maybe a teenage child uttered a harsh word against you years back that is still lingering in your heart, or a parent who is now deceased harmed you in some way. Pray and ask God's Spirit to enable you to offer mercy and forgiveness where you have not previously been able. If possible, let that person know of God's mercy and goodness in you and how you are now able to make things right again.

5. Listen to the biblical examples from Zechariah and James who call us as believers to care specifically for widows and orphans. Adopt a nursing home or a children's home and begin providing for these special people through your prayers, your time, and your assets. Be a Big Brother or Big Sister for a child with one or no parents. Notice the widows in your life and treat one to lunch or to a walk through a garden or a park. Give yourself in goodness.

6. Give away something of yours that you really value or that is important to you. Give it away for no other reason than to prevent greed from setting into your heart. Give away a car or a piece of jewelry or a special book or collectible. Give it to charity, give it to a friend, give it to your child or sibling. Experience the freedom of giving and the joy of goodness blossoming in your heart.

Faithfulness

"...the fruit of the Spirit is love, joy, peace, patience, kindness, goodness, faithfulness, gentleness, self-control..."

GALATIANS 5:22—23a

Faithfulness

"...the fruit of the Spirit is love, joy, peace, patience, kindness, goodness, *faithfulness*..."

"Faithfulness" is an old word. It comes from good stock, good parents, impressive grandparents and ancestors. Faithfulness, in fact, comes from God.

God. God who made a covenant with Abraham and said, "I will be faithful to you." God. God who made a covenant with Moses and the Israelites and said, "I will be faithful to you." God. God who made a covenant with the world by sending Jesus Christ and said, "In Him, I am faithful to you." God is faithful. God keeps His word. God does what He says. God makes good on His promises. God is true even when His people are not. "Faithfulness" is an old, old word. "Faithfulness" is a good word. It comes from God.

Maybe it is because "faithfulness" is such an old, old word that it now seems hopelessly old-fashioned and outdated. In America, right now, approximately 50 percent of marriages end in divorce. The idea of faithfulness has lost favor. We make promises to spouses, friends, and co-workers and then fail to follow through. A large percentage of adults believe that it is all right to be unfaithful to one's spouse, to commit adultery. Faithfulness seems like a relic, a thing of the past. Our celebrities revel in their unfaithfulness, appearing in one magazine with a new boyfriend this week, moving in with each other the following week, and then appearing again in a few months with a new relationship. And we all celebrate their desire to be "happy," all the while forgetting that faithfulness to God and faithfulness to one another is *the* way to happiness and life itself.

Faithfulness is of God. God is faithful, and He made us to be faithful. In fact, it is only when we learn the depths of faithfulness that we will become all that God intends us to be. He has expectations for us. When we are faithful to His expectations, we experience remarkable blessings.

Faithfulness is a fruit of God's Spirit because God is faithful to us. We will grow in faithfulness as His Spirit governs our lives. With the Holy Spirit, our hearts will take on an entirely new dimension and character. Our faithfulness will begin to reflect the faithfulness of God.

God's Faithfulness

Throughout my life and ministry, the Bible story that has had the greatest impact on me has been the story of the 99-year-old man named Abraham. God chooses Abraham to be the father of His very own people. He never gives the reason why He chooses Abraham, and He never provides much detail as to where Abraham will go. God is in charge, not Abraham. He simply tells Abraham to go where He leads, to an unnamed land that He will show him (Genesis 12:1-4).

Very simply, God teaches Abraham about faith. It is almost as though He is saying, "Trust me, and all the other details will be taken care of. If you trust me, I will be faithful." The rest of the book of Genesis—and really the rest of the entire Bible—tells the story of God's faithfulness to that very first promise to Abraham. That promise is God's promise to us.

Let's recall the words of that promise.

> Now the Lord said to Abram, "*Go* from your country and your kindred and your father's house *to the land that I will show you.* I will make of you a great nation, and I will bless you and make your name great so that you will be a blessing.

I will bless those who bless you and curse those who curse you; in you all the families of the earth shall be blessed." *So Abram went.*
GENESIS 12:1-4 NRSV

Later, in case Abraham worries, God says, "Do not be afraid, Abram, for I am your shield, and your reward shall be very great" (Genesis 15:1). God promises to give Abraham and Sarah (remember their advanced age!) a son who will be the beginning of God's chosen people forever. Surely God is crazy?! Children to a barren couple in their 90s? But God does just that.

God brought Abraham outside and said, "Look toward heaven, and count the stars if you are able to count them. So shall your descendants be."
GENESIS 15:5

Then, in Genesis 17, after Abraham has followed and obeyed God's direction to reach the unnamed land, God spells out His promises in even more detail. In essence, God says, "This is my covenant with you:
1) You will be the *ancestor* of a multitude of nations.
2) Your *name* shall be changed from Abram to Abraham.
3) I will make you exceedingly *fruitful.*
4) This will be an *everlasting* covenant.
5) I will give to you, and to your offspring after you, the *land* where you are now an alien, all the land of Canaan, for a *perpetual holding.*
6) *I will be their God.*
7) In return, you and your offspring will *circumcise* every male."

This one chapter of Genesis establishes the foundation for everything that is to follow. God's faithfulness to the promise is staggering and wonderful! The birth of Isaac. The stories of Jacob and Esau, of Joseph and his brothers. The gift of Moses who leads the Exodus of the people of Israel out of Egypt and into the Promised Land. The leadership of Joshua, the judges, Saul, David, and Solomon. The words of truth from the prophets. Over and over again, the Old Testament records God's faithfulness to Israel.

In the New Testament, God then extends His covenant beyond Israel to the entire world through the gift of His own Son, Jesus. Because God is faithful, Abraham becomes your father and mine when we become believers in Jesus. The book of Galatians lays that out before us. God's promise to Abraham becomes His promise to us because He is faithful.

God makes a simple covenant promise to Abraham and proves His faithfulness all the way through the Bible, through history, and into your life and mine! In other words, God is faithful and true. Faithfulness is simply part of God's character. Therefore, God's Spirit people, the followers of Jesus, will be faithful, too. Faithfulness is a fruit of God's Spirit.

Jesus on Faithfulness: Matthew 25:14-30

By the time we reach Matthew 25, Jesus is nearing the end of His time on earth.

His ministry with the disciples is drawing to a close, and He is preparing to face the cross. In these last days together, Jesus shares some very important things with His closest friends. He teaches them that the end will come when they least expect it, that they need to be watchful, and that He will come again in glory to judge all the world. Most of all, Jesus instructs His disciples and followers to be faithful. To be about the business that God made them for and to leave behind the things that are not of God. To be faithful: to tend to the work for which God created us.

Do you remember the parable of the talents discussed earlier in Matthew 25:14-30? Let's take another look at it from the perspective of the spiritual gift of *faithfulness*. Jesus tells us of a man who leaves for a long journey. Before he goes, he entrusts three of his servants with a large sum of money. The first servant with five talents (about $2Million in today's dollars), the second servant with two talents (about $900,000), and the third servant with one talent (about $450,000). After the man leaves, each of the servants is on his own until the master returns from his journey. The first two servants invest and trade and double their investments, but the third digs a hole in the ground and hides his master's money.

After a long time, the master returns and desires to learn what each of the servants has done with the large amount of money he has entrusted to them. When he learns that the first servant has turned five talents into ten and servant two has turned two talents into four, the master rejoices. To each of them, he says, "Well done, good and *faithful* servant; you have been *faithful* in a few things. I will put you in charge of many things. Enter into the joy of your master!" When he discovers that the third servant has done nothing more than bury his money and deliver no return or interest at all, the master rebukes him, calls him "worthless," and casts him out of the kingdom.

There are many things to notice about this parable. First, the master entrusts huge sums of money to his servants. In Jesus' time, servants often had tremendous amounts of freedom, particularly to do business on behalf of their master. In fact, it was not uncommon for an owner to entrust most of his business affairs and wealth to a handful of competent, business savvy servants.

Second, the master clearly expects a return for his investment. He wants his servants to manage his wealth, not merely bury it. When the master returns, he has a day of reckoning or accounting with his servants.

Third, the master generously rewards the two servants who produce a return. He praises them for their *faithfulness*. Because they have been faithful in this venture, the master gives them even more to manage and to tend. The master must be marvelously wealthy for he calls the sums he entrusted to the three servants only "a few things." Only the absurdly wealthy would consider millions of dollars small. How much more did he entrust to those two faithful servants?!

What does this tell us about God?

1) God is absurdly wealthy. In fact, all Creation belongs to Him. Everything that we see, possess, or touch belongs to Him. It is not ours. He alone is the Source. The world belongs to God. He made it and merely entrusts a portion of it to us for a short while. We are managers, stewards, servants; God is the Owner, the Source, the Master. He possesses; we merely manage.

2) *God is a Giver.* He gives each of us at least four things:

- ✐ Time—every moment and day is a gift from Him.
- ✐ Money and Possessions—all that we have is a gift from the Source. It is not ours. We merely manage it while we are here. When we die, God transfers responsibility for those resources and possessions to someone else.
- ✐ Talents—God invests skills, gifts, and abilities in each of us. Some receive musical gifts, others athletic skills, others craftsmanship, still others intellectual abilities. We do not earn those; we merely receive them from God. They are gifts.
- ✐ Faith—God instills within each of us a deep sense of who He is. We may hide it, deny it, or run from it, but still, deep within us, is the precious God-given gift of faith. He invites us to believe and to follow Him.

3) God expects a return on His investment in us. God does not bless us with life, time, money, talents, and faith for no reason. Quite the contrary. He expects, like the master in the parable, that we will utilize and manage all that He has given us to produce a return for Him.

What does that return look like? Jesus gives us two primary examples. First, in His final words to His disciples, Jesus gives them their great commission. "Go into all the world to make disciples of all nations, baptizing them in the name of the Father, and of the Son, and of the Holy Spirit, and teaching them to obey everything that I have commanded you" (Matthew 28:19-20).

God expects us to use our gifts to make disciples, to share the good news, to preach the Word, and to generate a harvest of lives changed by the gospel. He desires all the world to believe in Jesus Christ, to call Him "Lord," and to follow Him. Moreover, God expects to help make that kingdom mission happen. Our faithfulness in using our gifts will result in changed hearts, saved souls, new lives, and transformed relationships.

Second, Jesus again tells us that God expects us to care for the least, the last, and the lost. In fact, Jesus says that, at the judgment, God will note how we have cared for the naked, the hungry, the thirsty, the imprisoned, the stranger, and the sick (Matthew 25:31-46). God's heart seeks to bind up the wounds and hurts of the world, and His people will, too. Our faithfulness will result in healed wounds, mended hurts, and quenched appetites.

Very simply, God expects and desires His followers to love Him completely and to love our neighbors as we love ourselves. And to use every resource that He has invested in us to do so!

4) God encourages boldness and risk-taking. The master is not pleased with the servant who merely buries his investment in the ground and lives in fear. God encourages His people to take risks to share the gospel, to be bold in binding up the wounds of our neighbors. There is no such thing as a passive follower of Jesus. Followers follow! Following takes effort and work, and it may involve bold risks. In fact, it is a sin to be unwilling to venture out and act with what God has given us. He has invested vast sums in each of us, and He expects us to be faithful.

5) Jesus will return to "settle accounts." The day is coming when we shall see Jesus face to face. The day is coming when God will evaluate each of us for how we have managed His investment of time, money, talents, and faith. He expects us to be faithful, and we will ultimately answer for just how faithful we have been. That is why it is called the Judgment Day. Jesus will sit in judgment over us.

6) Excuses are not accepted. The third servant had lots of good reasons why he had failed to produce a return for God. He was scared; he was conservative. What he failed to understand was that no excuse is satisfactory. This is what we were made for: to love and serve God and to fulfill His mission in the world. There is *no* excuse because there is nothing else to do but to serve God. All else is but a shadow fading away. Our faithfulness is life itself.

The Examples of Carl and Linda

Anita and I met Carl when we were living in Connecticut and I was attending graduate school. Neither of us had spent much time around Catholic priests before, but my graduate work introduced us to some new friends. Carl was 89 years old when we met him, and I was a not-yet-30-year-old graduate student looking to get out of New England as quickly as I could. Our hearts were in Georgia and in the ministry. This time in Connecticut was but a short time of preparation for what God had in mind for us in the future.

Carl lived with a group of priests, one of whom studied with me and became a dear family friend. Carl had "retired" from the parish ministry of pastoring and preaching and had evolved into a new ministry of prayer. Each morning and each evening, he and the other priests gathered for prayer. Some attended as they could; Carl was *always* there.

Occasionally, after my classes, I would stop by the priory where the priests lived just to visit and check in. The priory was a home on the campus near the library, so it was directly on my route when walking back to our own house. I was a long way from home, and we had no one checking on us, so a few of the priests became our family in Connecticut. Although we were Methodists, they embraced our family as if we were related. In retrospect, in the kingdom, I guess I should have realized that they understood better than I that we are "kin."

More often than not, when I stopped by the priory, I would enter the little chapel for some quiet time before I walked the rest of the way back to our house. Each time I saw a number of different priests, but I always saw Carl.

Without fail, each time that I saw him, Carl asked about my health, which was not good at the time. He asked about my wife, who was and still is the finest one on earth, and he asked about my children. Every time. Without fail. And each time, without fail, he would say in his curmudgeonly New England Catholic priest kind of way, "Well, I've been praying for all of you." And I knew those were not empty words. They were heartfelt and deeply true.

Carl had spent sixty years pastoring churches before he retired to a ministry of prayer. When he retired, the secretaries and receptionists at his new church home and priory always knew that if someone needed a pastor in an emergency, Carl was the one to call—whether late at night or even early on Christmas morning. He was always ready and always willing and always eager to go. At eighty-nine years of age. Still faithful. Still true.

When I met him, Carl still wore the same clothes he had been wear-ing for nearly thirty years. He took his small pension each month and placed it in its entirety in the Poor Box, the small box at the front of the church where believers could give to help ease the pain and hurts of those around them. The Church where he lived provided the food and shelter that he actually needed, and Carl figured that was enough, so he gave all that he had. At eighty-nine years old. Still faithful. Still true.

I will never forget the day that I stopped by to pray and ran into Carl. I knew that he had been in continuous prayer for a friend of ours. When I saw him, his head was swollen with a large bruise on it. "Carl, what happened?" I asked. His matter-of-fact reply, "Oh, I was in the prayer chapel, and I fell asleep and hit my head on the railing." Faithful in prayer.

Carl had a deep loyalty to Christ that comes only with time. That loyalty had grown him to a level of faithfulness that most of us can only hope to attain. He was faithful in nearly every aspect of life. A life of faithful prayer, generous and sacrificial giving. A life of eager, willing, and joyful service. Carl and Jesus were good friends. The faithfulness of God flowed so deeply in Carl's veins that it nearly oozed out of his pores. Carl was faithful and true because God is faithful and true. Always.

Linda understands that also. Linda is an elderly woman in our con-gregation who has a ministry with babies and their families. Week in and week out, during the worship service Linda ministers to the small-est among us by rocking children and caring for them in the nursery. She has developed her own special prayer team to pray for each child who is baptized in our worship as well as that child's family. Each year, that prayer team hosts a dinner and party for all of those families to celebrate God's faithful grace in their lives.

At her advanced age, however, Linda's body has been experiencing the breakdowns and challenges that come naturally with aging. Her walking has become slow and laborious, requiring the assistance of a cane. Her body simply does not want to cooperate with her spirit. Each Sunday, it is hard work for her simply to arrive at the nursery.

So you can imagine my amazement on a stormy Sunday morning, as I prepared to preach at the eight o'clock service. I had already re-signed myself to the fact that on this day very few would attend church. It seemed obvious to me that most folks would awaken, hear and feel the rain, and decide it simply was not advantageous to get out in the rain to attend worship. As I looked out the window and prayed for that Sunday's worship, I saw a small car arrive and settle into the handicapped parking area. Slowly but surely, a woman emerged from the car, first cracking the car door, then opening an umbrella, then stepping out of her seat. Slowly but surely, Linda made her way into the nursery in the pouring down rain on a day when many folks far younger and healthier than she would not muster the spirit to worship God. But Linda knew and knows her calling. She loves God, and she loves God's children. She never considered anything else. Because Linda is faithful as God is faithful.

Faithfulness is a fruit of God's Spirit.

Growing a Life of Faithfulness

1. Set measurable goals. What do you think that God wants you to do with your life? Establish three to five goals that reflect the harvest you think God desires from your life. Reflect on how you can use your time, talents, money, and faith to generate these results. What can you do this week to help make it happen?

2. Claim your strengths and gifts that God has uniquely invested in you. Only you have the strengths and gifts that are yours and which God wants to use for His kingdom. Claim those. They are yours. Don't try to imitate or claim the gifts of others. God gifted and made you the way you are for a reason. Claim those gifts and strengths and use them for Him. He will be faithful when you do.

3. Remember whom you serve in everything you do for one day. God is the Source. He gave the gifts. He is the Owner and the Master. You serve Him. Never be seduced into thinking that your gifts belong to you; they are God's. Never be tempted to use your gifts for your gain or glory: they are for God's kingdom and glory. Serve Him faithfully in all that you do, and you will be amazed.

4. Remember and embrace the truth of John Wesley's teaching on faithfulness in financial affairs. Wesley, the great English preacher and leader of the eighteenth century, earned roughly $65 per year early in his ministry and soon found that he could live on just that amount. So he resolved always to use any monies that he earned over that amount to give to God's mission in the world. Later in his ministry, when his writings were widely published and distributed, Wesley earned more than $3,000 per year, but he still continued to live on $65. He summed up what he learned:

A. *Earn all you can* (1 Timothy 6:17-18)—without giving your
heart away to it
- Not at the expense of your body, mind or health
- Not at expense of neighbor (body, mind or well-being)
- Use honest hard work
- Use all diligence—lose no time, for you have none to
spare

B. *Save all you can* (Hebrews 13:5)
- Simplicity is a virtue
- Don't seek to satisfy your every whim, taste, thought, or
fancy
- Don't squander what you have on superfluous, expen-
sive, unuseful stuff
- The more passions are indulged, the more they increase
- Don't weigh yourself down with stuff. Jesus said, "Come,
follow me."
- Don't seek to impress others but simply to provide for
self and family

C. *Give all you can*—use possessions effectively and faithfully
for kingdom purposes (Luke 6:38; 2 Corinthians 9:6-8;
Galatians 6:7-8)
- You are a steward not an owner—soul, body, worldly
goods, talents, and mind all belong to God
- Provide for self and family's needs
- Then give all that you can—not 10 percent, $^1/_3$ or even
$^1/_2$, but all that is God's.
- Questions to ask when considering any expense:
  1) Am I acting according to the character of a steward
  of the Lord's goods?
  2) Am I acting in obedience to the Word of God?
  3) Can I offer this expense as a sacrifice to God through
  Jesus?
  4) Do I think that this work will generate God's favor
  at the resurrection judgment?

Gentleness

"...the fruit of the Spirit is love, joy, peace, patience, kindness, goodness, faithfulness, gentleness, self-control..."

GALATIANS 5:22—23a

Chapter VIII

Gentleness

"...the fruit of the Spirit is love, joy, peace, patience, kindness, goodness, faithfulness, *gentleness*..."

Anger. Temper.

I have to admit that these two words describe the qualities that I find least attractive in people. We just are not very pretty to look at when we are angry and out of control. Veins popping, eyes bulging, faces turning red. To be honest, when I meet someone with an explosive temper, I usually try my best to avoid being around that person. Tempers are often frightening and can even be dangerous. Explosive tempers do not look good on Christians especially. Christians, seeking to live in the Spirit of God, simply should not wear that kind of demeanor.

Now let me be clear: that does not mean that Christians should be pushovers or doormats. Quite the contrary. They should be strong and courageous. When you know who you are and to whom you belong, a gentle strength naturally begins to flow out of that knowledge. Why? Because gentleness flows from the strong, bold Spirit of God. Gentleness is a sign of strength, not weakness, in the same way that angry bullying is a sign of weakness, not strength. Christians are free to be gentle because we live for a purpose higher than merely getting our own way in this world. Instead, believers get satisfaction and pleasure in seeing and knowing God's way.

If gentleness is a fruit of God's Spirit, and He promises that fruit to us as His children, what then does the Bible say about gentleness? Four things.

Four Qualities of Biblical Gentleness

1) *At ease*

First of all, a believer is at ease with himself and with God. To know Christ is to be set right with God. We quit trying to do things our way and begin to do them God's way. We can never be gentle until we are right with God. In Christ, we begin to live life like it is intended. He puts us at ease with the Lord.

Christians are at ease because the stress and tension of living are relieved by the Spirit of God. When we are operating on our own strength and our own agenda, we are tense, uptight, struggling. Things are never quite right. Nothing feels settled. When we are living in the Spirit of God, operating on His strength and His agenda, we find a relaxing freedom in knowing that we are living in His will rather than our own. The worries and tension fade away. Gentleness is the result.

Hear the basic encouragement of Romans 8:31b: "If God is for us, who can be against us?" When we are on God's side, many of our worries and fears fade away. In the end, we realize that we are His. We belong to Him. He stands with us. Tensions are reduced. Gentleness is the result. Christians are free to be gentle and at ease because we know that God stands with us.

The New Testament Greek word for "gentleness" literally means "to have a tamed neck." What a great image! A Christian is not like a mule, stubborn and resistant. That is how we live before we are "in Christ." Before Christ, we fight and resist, always struggling against our untamed passions and habits. Some are controlled by anger and addictions, others by depression and despair. Some obsessively seek the admiration and praise of other people and end up hopelessly enslaved to their need for approval. Before Christ, we are not at ease. We are restless.

However, once we are "in Christ," we begin to be tamed and settled. Our spirit now cooperates with the Spirit of God. Instead of finding tension and harshness in continually fighting against God, we now find the gentleness of obeying Him and walking in His way. Rather than straining to seek the approval of others, we have been approved by God. We are at ease. That is what we were made for in the first place!

Brian may be the most settled, gentle person I have ever known. I became friends with him at a monastery where I spend a day in prayer each month. Brian leads that monastery's monks and, for a time, agreed to meet with me periodically for spiritual friendship, conversation, and guidance. On nearly every occasion, I would always arrive frazzled, tense, and anxious about the world's worries. And each time I would find Brian completely at ease and greeting me with a divine calmness. Through the years of Brian's prayer, devotion, leadership, and service, the Holy Spirit had so invaded his life that everything about him radiated an "at easeness." Patiently listening, calmly smiling, faithfully praying with me, Brian would inevitably stir a gentleness within me that had not existed before. His gentle ease led me closer to Jesus.

2) *Controlled*

Secondly, a believer keeps her anger and her passions under control. A believer is not controlled by his overeating or by his obsession with continually acquiring more worldly "stuff." In this way, gentleness is linked to the fruit of self-control. The Spirit does not produce explosive, out-of-control, violent, scary people; the Spirit brings control.

God's Spirit does not lead to the overindulgence of every fleshly whim or emotional desire. For example, anger is not always bad. Of course, there are times when we are right to be angry. When criminals attack an innocent victim, or when a child is abused, our anger is justifiable. However, anger can easily cross into dangerous territory when it seeks to hurt others or to avenge. A Christian's anger, even when it is righteous anger, is always tempered with love and mercy. Out-of-control anger is sin. Anger may be justifiable; sin is not.

One of the most unpleasant experiences in my life came when I had no choice but to serve in a ministry alongside a person whose anger was out of control. His explosiveness and rage in every situation demoralized volunteers and created a sense of fear throughout the ministry. Anyone who served or shared in that ministry was terrified of being the victim of one of his outbursts or tantrums. Sadly, over time, his lack of gentleness slowly squeezed the joy and the purpose out of that ministry.

In contrast, Christians control their passions rather than allowing their passions to control them. Only the Holy Spirit can make that possible because the Bible is clear that before we are Christians, we can't help but be slaves to our passions. Listen to Ephesians 2:3: "All of us once lived…in the passions of our flesh, following the desires of our flesh and senses." In other words, before we met Jesus, we gave in to our passions and desires. Now we give in to Christ and His Spirit. We gain control through the Spirit of gentleness.

3) *Humility*

Humility is the first cousin of gentleness. They go hand in hand. When our pride is held in check and our ego is contained, humility results. Humility lives at the heart of God. Humility understands and remembers that other people matter just as much as we do. God loves each one of us just the same. Whether we are rich or poor, young or old, handsome or homely, God loves us immeasurably *and* equally. Knowing that one basic fact builds the foundation of humility. Say it aloud: "I am just as valuable to God as any other person." At the same time, remember: "Any other person is just as important to God as I am."

We are arrogant when we view ourselves too highly and others too poorly. There is no gentleness there—only pride. Humility lies in knowing who we are: a child loved by God.

Humility leads directly to gentleness. Gentleness is not proud or puffed up. Gentleness treats other people like we ourselves want to be treated in return. A gentle believer cares as much about his neighbor as he does about himself. Gentleness seeks humbly to make other people look better. A gentle Christian sincerely and earnestly seeks the best for the other people around her. Most importantly, gentleness seeks God's salvation for others.

Gentleness is particularly important as we share our faith with non-believers. A harsh, judgmental spirit will usually result in rejection and dismissal. The Bible reminds us in 2 Timothy 2:24-25:

> The Lord's servant must not be quarrelsome but kindly to everyone, an apt teacher, patient, *correcting opponents with gentleness*. God may perhaps grant that they will repent and come to know the truth. (NRSV)

A gentle spirit allows others to approach you, to hear the truth, and to ask questions. Harshness and severity close off the conversation too soon. Gentleness creates room for people around you to come and meet Jesus through you. Harshness slams the door quickly. Cultivating a gentle spirit will bear fruit for God's kingdom in the lives of people around you. Leading other people into the presence of Jesus: that is quite an incentive!

4) *Forgiving*

Finally, gentleness is rooted in forgiveness. Gentle believers do not hold grudges. Instead, they are molded by the hand of the Lord who is forgiving and gentle. Once we realize just how much God has forgiven us, we cannot help but try to reflect that same forgiveness to the people in our lives. A humble self-awareness of our own sins leads to a growing ability to forgive others. That is gentleness of spirit. We do not treat others harshly while asking God to treat us gently. Quite the contrary. The closer we are drawn to God, the more forgiving and gentle we become.

Now that is very different from a world which seeks vengeance and rejects forgiveness. We live in an unforgiving, grudge-holding world. For example, the Scottish government opened a new $4.5 million Tourist Visitor Center in 2002 at Glencoe, where 310 years ago, members of the Campbell clan slaughtered thirty-eight members of the MacDonald clan. When the site opened, Roddy Campbell was introduced as the center's director. An angry Hector MacDonald responded to the announcement of Mr. Campbell's appointment by saying to reporters, "Don't get me wrong. I have nothing against the Campbells, but I would not stay a night in the company of one." The newswriter covering the story wrote, "There are still some very strong feelings about the massacre here." What an understatement! More than ten generations have passed, but members of these two families still cling to a 310-year-old grudge. That may be a world record for grudge-holding!

However, where the world is harsh, bitter, and cynical, the believer gently extends the hand of forgiveness and the spirit of gentleness. Christians may be *in* the world, but we always know that we are not *of* it.

My children have taught me this lesson better than anyone else. Their ability to forgive and forget regularly amazes me. When I am harsh or sharp-tongued, they are quick to forgive me gently and move forward. They release their grudges rather than bear the weight of carrying them. One daughter routinely points out to her parents what she calls "the two most helpful words" in the English language when she reminds us, "Nobody's perfect." My own daughters' witness explains to me in part why Jesus tells us to receive the kingdom like children. Gentleness and forgiveness often come easily to them.

Adults can embody the gentleness of forgiveness, too. Do you remember the story of Joseph and his brothers in Genesis? Joseph's brothers are so jealous of his gifts and abilities that they sell him into slavery to get rid of him. Over time, the slave, Joseph, rises to power under the pharaoh in Egypt. After years of separation, his brothers come to Egypt and meet Joseph but fail to recognize him. At last, Joseph has his chance for revenge. Remarkably, however, rather than getting even for an old grudge, he instead offers his betraying brothers a full measure of forgiveness. Some of the verses in Genesis here are among the most powerful in the Bible.

Joseph has grown so close to the Lord that he is able to see His hand at work throughout his life, even in his brothers' act of selling him into slavery. God has shaped his spirit with such gentleness that Joseph is able to tell his brothers, "So it was not you who sent me into Egypt but God; He has made me a father to pharaoh, and lord of all his house, and ruler over all the land of Egypt" (Genesis 45:8).

Moreover, Joseph combines his forgiveness with generosity. He provides for his brothers and their families, giving them food and shelter during their time of suffering and famine (Genesis 45:11). Despite all of this gentleness, his brothers later still worry that Joseph will not be able to forgive them (Genesis 50:15). And Joseph again amazes them with his spirit of gentleness. "Even though you intended it for harm, God intended it for good...So do not fear; I will provide for you and your children" (Genesis 50:20).

Joseph is proof that God's Spirit brings a gentleness that expresses itself in forgiveness as well as in generosity.

This same spirit of gentleness can take root in us. When we discover the misdeeds or failures of a brother or sister in Christ, God calls us to seek to restore rather than reject that friend in Christ.

> My friends, if anyone is detected in a transgression, you who have received the Spirit should restore such a one in a spirit of gentleness.
> GALATIANS 6:1 NRSV

Rejection is easy while restoration is hard work. Joseph shows us the way as he faces his brothers years after their betrayal of him. And he does so with gentleness, grace, mercy, and love. Clearly, restoration and healing are possible only through God. His Spirit alone can provide that kind of healing and mold us into a people of forgiveness. He desires for us to be a people of gentleness.

A Goal of Gentleness: Leading Others to Salvation

> In your hearts, sanctify Christ Jesus as Lord. Always be ready to make your defense to anyone who demands from you an accounting for the hope that is in you; yet do it with *gentleness and reverence*.
> 1 PETER 3:15-16

Here, Peter makes our aim clear: holy hearts. Hearts made holy by Christ. Holy hearts with a God-given hope. He also makes it clear that our gentleness can help other people meet our Lord, Jesus Christ. What an opportunity: to have our own gentleness help lead others to salvation. That is a truly Christian way of looking at gentleness.

Too often, the world is full of arrogant, self-righteous Christians who are smug and secure in their own salvation, and also eager to point out the sins of the people around them. Like the Christian who listens to sermons so that he can tell others how good they ought to be while never looking at himself in the mirror. Or the Christian who sees herself as the world's police officer patroling the globe, hoping to point out everyone else's wrongs. In these verses, Peter clearly envisions just the opposite. A Christian is a gentle person who loves others and graciously shares what she has, especially her hope in Christ. That is who Christians are: humble, caring people with holy hearts that love God. Holy hearts rooted in gentleness.

Don is a highly effective evangelist. However, he never preaches from pulpits. Instead, Don gently tells the people around him about Jesus. He allows the Holy Spirit to make him a gentle person, easily approached and readily befriended. Don seeks to meet people where they are. He relates to the people in his neighborhood, in his workplace, and in his relationships in a way that is highly effective at leading people to Jesus Christ. Don never argues about the truth, but rather he patiently listens to the other person's thoughts and then gently replies with the truth of the gospel. He responds to confrontation with a smile and an outstretched hand. Don is no pushover; on the contrary, he is quite firm in who he is and what he believes. But the reason that hundreds of persons around him have come to faith in Christ is because of his gentleness. Quite simply, he carries a gentle heart that loves people and he remembers his God-given opportunity: to let his gentleness lead other people to the living waters of Jesus.

The Gentleness Model of Jesus

For a model of gentleness, of course, the supreme example is Jesus. Consider the events of His ministry. Discover the awesome power and strength that lies underneath His gentleness.

Walk with Him through the Gospel of Luke as He:

- Touches and heals a *leper* who desperately begs to be delivered from a deadly disease that prevents other people from touching or associating with him (5:12-16).
- Teaches His followers to "Love your *enemies*, do good to those who hate you, bless those who curse you, pray for those who abuse you" (6:27-31).

- Consoles a *widow* whose son has just died and then brings the boy back to life (7:11-17).

- Rebukes the Pharisee who chastises the well-known *sinful woman* as she kisses and anoints Jesus' feet. Jesus then forgives her sins and sends her forth with His blessing (7:36-50).

- Demonstrates to His arguing disciples where true greatness lies by embracing and welcoming a small *child* (9:46-48).

- Tells the parable of the good *Samaritan* whose gentleness, generosity, and mercy overflowed and expected no repayment. Note how Jesus tells the lawyer, "Go and do likewise" (10:25-37).

- Lays hands on a *woman crippled* for eighteen years even though the religious leaders criticized His doing so on the Sabbath (13:10-17).

- Welcomes the little *children* whom His own disciples are turning away (18:15-17).

- Endures His *trial* before Pilate and Herod, His *humiliation* from the crowd, and His *death* on the cross (23:1-43).

- Instructs the *women weeping* by the side of the road as He walks the agonizing road to Calvary, saying to them, "Don't weep for me, but weep for yourselves and your children" (23:28).

- Loves even the *two criminals* dying on either side of Him at the cross. Listen as He says to the believing one, "Truly, I tell you, today you will be with me in paradise" (23:43).

The strength and power of Jesus are expressed in how He faces His enemies with gentleness. He encounters the weak and the outcast with gentleness. His courage provides the platform for an extraordinary outpouring of gentleness even when He is suffering and at the point of death.

Clearly, gentleness has tremendous power. Of course it does! Gentleness is a fruit of God's Spirit, and there is no power like that of the Holy Spirit. Come, Holy Spirit, come. Fill our lives with your power and your gentleness.

Growing a Life of Gentleness

1. Learn to count to ten. That is the single best step for learning to control your anger and your temper and may well be your most productive way to grow in gentleness. When your emotional temperature rises, when the temptation to lash out is strongest, counting to ten allows yourself the time and space to back off. Your first instinct may not be your best.

2. Exercise. Science has taught us for decades that regular, rigorous exercise releases endorphins into our bodies. These agents calm the body and still the mind and soul. A calmer body and soul provide fertile ground for gentleness to grow.

3. Write a letter of forgiveness or make restitution for damages caused in order to eliminate the grudges you hold, as well as those held against you. Old hurts and wounds have a remarkable power over us. They build up like water behind a dam, slowly increasing over time to a level that can no longer be held back. Take the difficult steps to mend old hurts, to bind up old wounds. Take the first step. Write a letter to forgive or to seek forgiveness. If the offender is now dead, write the letter anyway. It will cleanse you and set you free to treat others gently rather than harshly. If you have hurt someone or something, find a way to make restitution. Pay back the debt in some way. Remove the bonds and shackles that prevent you from living with gentleness. Be made whole!

4. Skip caffeine for a day. Marvel at the gentleness that emerges in your day. Take the edge off. Watch as your pace slows, your attention allows you to notice those around you, and you interact with a new level of gentleness.

5. Get a massage. Experience the healing grace of touch to release the tensions that bind you. Early in my ministry, I received the gift of a free massage, or body therapy. Once I overcame my fear

(not to mention all of the misinformation I associated with such experiences), this gift became a tremendous blessing to me and my ministry, as well as in my own life in the Spirit. The tensions and the stresses that I so often kept inside me had become a part of my body. Through masssage, I was able to release the unproductive grudges, tensions, and hurts that prevented me from the gentleness to which the Spirit calls us.

6. Volunteer in the nursery of your church. Play with a baby. Spend time with the vulnerable, the innocent, and the simple so that the Spirit of gentleness can stir deep within you. Tom is a disabled man, frustrated by his body's unwillingness to allow him to do the things he would like to do with his life and for God. He has found his place in the world by volunteering several days per week at a Christian early learning center, spending hours on the floor and in the rocker with infants and toddlers. His own spirit, so frustrated and aggravated by his physical disability, is renewed each day with the gentleness of being God's agent around the smallest and most vulnerable among us.

7. Visit the elderly residents of a nursing home. You are indebted to them as they helped to lay the foundation on which your life is built. You will not be able to offer much besides your presence. That is the point. Have no agenda other than God's, and watch your gentleness grow.

8. Spend time with the mentally ill. The world avoids them and often separates them from society. Bridge the gap. Gently love someone whom no one else notices. Listen, play, care. Grow in gentleness.

9. Serve a child who is hurting. As a Big Brother or Big Sister, as a foster parent, as a volunteer in a children's hospital. Serve a small person who cannot do anything for you but receive what you offer. The gift of being able only to give and not receive will grow your gentleness. The Spirit will reshape your heart.

10. If you have the gift of caring or compassion, serve as a "Stephen minister." Stephen ministers are thoroughly trained to provide quality, meaningful care for someone who is hurting. Allow the gentleness of the Spirit to flow through you to the hurting and broken.

11. Eat lunch at the hospital and make a quick visit to see a patient there. Bring a flower. Brighten someone's day. As you notice the harshness and coldness of the hospital, you will become more gentle in order to soften the heavy load of the person you visit.

Self-Control

"...the fruit of the Spirit is love, joy, peace, patience, kindness, goodness, faithfulness, gentleness, self-control..."

GALATIANS 5:22—23a

Self-Control

"...the fruit of the Spirit is love, joy, peace, patience, kindness, goodness, faithfulness, gentleness, *self-control*..."

Question: What usually makes the difference between a life that is barren and empty versus a life that is full of the fruitful blessings of God?

Answer: Self-control

More often than not, self-control determines whether you will have a life that is fruit-full and full of God. Without self-control, such a life is only a dream. In fact, self-control is the key to enjoying the other eight fruit of the Spirit. Self-control allows us the opportunity *to choose to do* those things that are healthy and helpful and *to choose not to do* those things that are harmful and destructive. Self-control helps us to be open to God's Spirit and work with Him rather than resisting Him. Self-control helps us resist the temptations that lead away from God and fruit-full living. Self-control is a good thing, and it is a God thing.

God's gift of free will to each of us means that we can choose to work with or against His Spirit in our lives. And self-control is perhaps the greatest tool available to us to cooperate with God's work in our lives. We can choose to exercise self-control or abandon it. More than any other fruit of the Spirit, this is one fruit we can control. Even better, through the wise use of this one fruit we can cultivate the other eight fruit of the Spirit in our lives. Self-control can lead to a greater abundance of the other fruit in us.

At the same time, self-control can be a tough fruit to bear as we are surrounded by a culture that discourages its use. In fact, our world often encourages a total lack of it! Consider the utter lack of self-control that fills our lives as we watch television talk shows such as Jerry Springer where guests revel in being out of control, or as we read about the serial sexual relationships of politicians and celebrities who often seem to jump from bed to bed almost by the week.

In a world like this, how do we muster the strength to have self-control? How do we learn to master our own passions and temptations in order to live in God's Spirit and to enjoy the fruit of that Spirit? Good news! The Bible gives a marvelous prescription for how to grow a life full of self-control.

5 Biblical Steps toward Self-Control

1) *Decide what you really want.*

It seems so simple and obvious, but the place to begin is by asking yourself, "What do I really want in life?" What matters most in your life? If you could choose only one priority for your life, what would it be? A loving spouse, the blessings of children, abundant riches, a successful career?

Before you decide, remember the words of Jesus: "Seek ye *first* the kingdom of God and His righteousness, and all these things shall be added unto you" (Matthew 6:33).

Or remember the ten commandments, where God's first law for living says, "You shall have *no* other gods before me" (Exodus 20:3).

God makes it clear. He is the priority for life. He comes first. He is number one. With that decision made, all other blessings and fruit begin to flow in our lives. Without that decision, our lives will shipwreck on the rocks of our own wishes and ambitions.

For example, Ken Caminiti's key priority was a successful baseball career and all that went with it. He wanted to be the best. He wanted to earn the adoration of crowds and the immense financial rewards of athletic success, and he was willing to do anything to achieve that. *Anything.* A decade later, Ken's body is so severely damaged from the steroids he chose to use to make himself more successful that he is out of baseball altogether. His marriage is ruined. His reputation is sullied from the arrests for cocaine possession and drug abuse that he used to relieve the stress of desiring success at all costs. Ken Caminiti won the MVP award in baseball, but his decision to be the best not only shortchanged his physical health, it also cost him nearly everything else in his life. Even more sadly, as chronicled by a June 2002 issue of *Sports Illustrated,* we look around and witness ongoing Congressional hearings and a nationwide discussion of why so many people are willing to sell out their bodies, health, and futures for a $10 million salary and a fleeting cheer from the crowd. It is easy to see that poor choices can quickly lead to a life that is out of control.

However, the examples of not choosing what we want wisely are not always that extreme. Sue merely wanted happiness. She desired happiness more than anything else. In her mind, job stress, marital strains, the demands of children, the pressures of family all prevented her happiness, so she began to look for it in other ways. In the end, Sue landed in an alcohol rehabilitation facility for her addiction to a substance she hoped could help her escape those pressures and give her the happiness she so desperately longed for. Her time in the rehabilitation center finally helped her to see that making a poor choice of what she really wanted in life had led to an out of control life. Sue had mistaken a good feeling, a quickened pulse rate, and high emotions for a meaningful and happy life.

Again, the point is simple: if you deeply desire the fruit of the Spirit, choose God above all else. If you want a life that bears fruit like love, joy, peace, patience, kindness, and goodness, make up your mind to desire Him first, above everything and everyone else.

2) *Give your life over to Him.*

After choosing God as your first priority, give your life completely over to Him. Completely. Every aspect. Every part. Every day. Completely. In doing so, you will discover the joy of being governed by Him. Having His Spirit govern and control your life. The Bible describes it this way:

> I have been crucified with Christ and I no longer live, but Christ lives in me. The life I live in the body, I live by faith in the Son of God, who loved me and gave Himself for me.
> GALATIANS 2:20 NIV

What a marvelous passage of Scripture! In fact, this single verse may well be the crucial key to self-control. Make Jesus the Lord of life, and He will live in us. We will live life in a new way, by faith in Him. It is important to see that the apostle Paul writes this verse just a few chapters before he teaches us about the fruit of the Spirit. This verse sets the stage for fruit-full living by showing us how God works.

First, Jesus gave Himself for me. He loved me first.

Second, I accept that love and make Him Lord of my life. I put my past ways behind me and am co-crucified with Him. My old way of doing things is put to death and replaced by His love.

Third, Christ becomes the governor of my life and He directs my life through His Holy Spirit.

This is the goal of the Christian life—to have Jesus Christ, through His Holy Spirit, directing and governing every part of my life. He is not *one part* of my life; He is *life itself.* With this basic step of faith in place, we are set free from our own ways to discover the mighty power of God in our lives!

Good news! When the Holy Spirit begins to rule and to reign in our lives, self-control will naturally follow.

3) *Seek His Spirit and His counsel in all that you do.*

Self-control is a daily, step-by-step process of learning to have self-control in what we say, how we act, what we eat, and where we go. Step by step, day by day, that is how we give our life over to Him. And the more life that is given over to Him, the more Spirit-filled self-control is available to us.

How does this happen? Through the Holy Spirit whom God promises to share with us step by step, day by day. God desires, most of all, to walk beside us each day, directing our steps and decisions, guiding our hearts and our minds. He tells us that over and over again in Scripture.

a) The Holy Spirit governs us when we *pray.*

Prayer is marrow. Marrow is where your body manufactures blood, where your blood cells are produced—the blood cells that are life itself. In other words, marrow produces life at its most basic level and also generates defense for your body and blood against diseases and any other attackers of life. Webster's defines marrow as the "innermost, essential, choicest part." It is simple: you cannot survive without marrow.

Prayer is our spiritual marrow. It is the marrow of our souls, the innermost, essential, choicest part of our life with God. Prayer generates life in our souls, and it provides defense against the things that attack the soul. Prayer is where we communicate with God, live in God, are formed by God, and pay attention to Him. Prayer plugs our soul into God Himself.

As our souls become connected to God in prayer, one saint of the church said that we then learn to shift from what we want to what God wants. And therein lies the heart of self-control: learning to desire what God wants rather than what we want. Prayer makes God's counsel available to us. That is why the Bible teaches us to "pray without ceasing" (1 Thessalonians 5:17).

b) The Holy Spirit guides us when we *immerse ourselves in the Bible.*

Read the Word and be amazed at how your relationship with God grows and matures, at how your conversion deepens and your self-control will increase. Why? Because

> All Scripture is God-breathed and is useful for teaching, for reproof, for correction, and for training in righteousness, so that everyone who belongs to God may be proficient, equipped for every good work
> 2 TIMOTHY 3:16-17

Scripture is God-breathed. It is spoken by God, breathed out by Him. In other words, when we spend time in the Word, we spend time with God. He meets us there. And the results are staggering! Something happens to us and in us. We are taught, reproved, corrected, trained for righteousness, and equipped for good works. We are conformed to God. The Scriptures are so saturated with His Spirit that we are changed by our study in them. We are changed to have the mind of Christ. Scripture helps us be co-crucified with Christ and to live in Him alone. Again, the result is a greater measure of self-control.

That's why God invites you and me to form a habit with the Bible. The Old Testament puts it this way:

> Hear, O Israel: The Lord is our God; the Lord alone. You shall love the Lord your God with all your heart, and with all your soul, and with all your strength. Keep these words that I am commanding you today in your hearts. Recite them to your children and talk about them when you are home and when you are away, when you lie down and when you get up. Bind them as a sign on your hand, fix them as an emblem on your forehead, and write them on the doorposts of your house and on your gates.
> DEUTERONOMY 6:4-9

God's Word is clear: Form a Bible habit. Saturate your life with the Bible, because then the Spirit will saturate you.

c) The Holy Spirit directs us through the *support and encouragement of godly friends.*

Twelve Step programs, such as Alcoholics Anonymous, have known this basic concept for years. If you want to find change in your life, change your playgrounds and playmates. Recovering alcoholics are encouraged to quit hanging around people and places which encourage them to drink or to give in to temptation. The application of this concept to our desire for self-control is obvious. If friends or places lead to your being out of control, then change friends and places. To cultivate self-control, find the support of other believers who are also seeking to grow in the fruit of God's Spirit. Their encouragement will strengthen your own desires and heart.

Learn to rely on these folks and gather their wisdom as God speaks through them. The Bible teaches time and again of the crucial role that our fellow believers can and should play in our own spiritual growth. In the book of Acts alone, the believers meet regularly with one another for prayer, worship, Bible study, and encouragement (e.g., Acts 2:42-47; 4:32-37; 13:1-3; 14:21-28). Believers help one another discern what the Spirit of God desires and where the Spirit is leading.

Being a Christian is a team sport. We are a part of a greater community. The Holy Spirit speaks to us through the lives and mouths of our fellow believers.

4) *Replace old habits with new ones.*

As we learn to desire God first, to give our lives completely over to Him, and to seek His counsel and Spirit in all that we do, we will slowly replace our old habits with new ones. God's governance will give us strength to resist habits that used to control us and the areas where we lack self-control. His Spirit will take over and our new habits will become holy habits.

These holy habits will allow God to change us and form us. Holy habits require effort, they will take work. God's grace is not cheap. It is not always easy. But the Holy Spirit meets us there.

This is what the Bible talks about when the apostle Paul says,

> Do you not know that in a race the runners all compete, but only one receives the prize? Run in such a way that you may win it. Athletes exercise self-control in all things; they do it to receive a perishable crown but we an imperishable one. So I do not run aimlessly, nor do I box as though beating the air; but I punish my body and enslave it.
>
> 1 CORINTHIANS 9:24-27

Successful athletes maintain a disciplined, self-controlled regimen of workouts and diet. They learn to put aside those habits that will prevent their success. They learn to develop habits that will advance their strength and prowess. The same is true for the spirit we have as believers. To advance our spiritual strength, we will learn to develop holy habits that place us under the influence of God's Spirit.

On July 23, 1996, in downtown Atlanta, Georgia, little Kerri Strug was taking her final turn at the vault in hopes of winning a gold medal, a gold she had not attained four years earlier in the Olympics. Also a gold medal the women's gymnastics team had never attained in history. And she was the final hope.

You probably remember the picture of Kerri's vaulting over the horse with severe ligament and tendon damage in her ankle. She struggled valiantly under great personal pain, and she nailed the flawless vault to propel the women to gold as a team for the first time in history. Kerri Strug instantly rocketed into our memories and into remarkable fame. Magazines and television spots all showed that image of her standing there, courageous and victorious. Commentators and columnists remarked that she had become a national hero overnight—or so it seemed.

What none of those writers or announcers mentioned much was that Kerri had been training for more than twelve years—seven hours a day, six days a week. Training relentlessly with discipline, vigor, and passion—for twelve years to be ready for that one moment and to become an "overnight" sensation!

The Bible reminds us in 1 Corinthians 9:24-27 that you and I are seeking not some gold medal that will be forgotten over the years, but rather an eternal crown, a crown of glory with the King of glory, Jesus Christ. Just as this world's athletes train to prepare for victory, you and I work at growing closer to God. We train. We develop holy habits like prayer, Scripture, and godly friends in order to grow us forward as believers. We train, and it will be worth it. We will gain entry into the kingdom of God and become a part of His heavenly chorus—forever! And our holy habits now will pay off richly then.

5) *Follow Him one day at a time.*

Finally, life and the Bible teach us that self-control will not emerge in us overnight. It takes time. It grows daily. God's Spirit takes over and begins to govern us. Change occurs in spurts, in small increments, in huge leaps, but always over time. To try to decide today to have God-governance or self-control for every day the rest of our lives is to decide to fail. Instead, seek God anew each day. Seek Him each hour. Let the years to come take care of themselves. Decide for Him just for today. Self-control will soon follow.

Peter put it this way:

> For this very reason, you must make every effort to support your faith with goodness, and goodness with knowledge, and knowledge with *self-control*, and *self-control* with endurance, and endurance with godliness.
> 2 PETER 1:5-6 NRSV

Bit by bit, day by day, faith brings goodness which brings knowledge, then self-control and godliness. The change may be barely noticeable at first, but over time, however, the transformation is amazing and wonderful.

One wise man of the church said, "How does an apple ripen? It just sits in the sun." Thomas Merton reflected that a small green apple cannot ripen in one night by tightening all its muscles and squinting its eyes in order to miraculously find itself the next morning a large, ripe and juicy red apple. In the same way, our transformation in Christ Jesus does not occur overnight. It takes time. It takes effort. It takes self-control.

When you do these five biblical steps, be sure to look around you. Love, joy, and peace will soon begin to pop up in your flower beds. Patience, kindness, and goodness will begin to blossom in your orchard. Faithfulness and gentleness will sprout up in your garden. And they'll all be fertilized by the same thing: self-control.

The key to self-control is to desire God. To yearn for His face and His presence. To have a heart for pleasing Him and serving Him only. If you want to look like Jesus, it begins with self-control. If you want to grow in God's Spirit, it begins with self-control.

Self-control is a fruit of God's Spirit.

Growing a Life of Self-Control

1. Add a regular prayer time to your life. Perhaps a daily quiet time. Perhaps a monthly day of retreat at a monastery or park. Perhaps a weekly meeting as a part of the prayer ministry at your church. Claim time on a regular basis for absolute time with God. Seek His Spirit and counsel. Seek His strength for self-control. Grow in His Spirit and grace. Spend time with Him.

2. Add a Scripture habit to your life. Join a regular weekly or monthly Bible study at your church. Buy a copy of the One Year Bible and use it to work your way through the Scriptures. Listen to the Bible on tape as a part of your daily commute. Participate in an intensive Bible study at church or with friends for several weeks. Find a way to have Scripture fill your life. Feast on the Word. Live in the Spirit.

3. Cultivate godly friends who will encourage your self-control. Become part of a prayer team, a Bible study group, a mission team, a musical ensemble, or a neighborhood group who will offer wisdom, encouragement, and strength for you just as you do for them. Find friends who seek self-control and godliness. Live in the Spirit with them.

4. Give up a harmful habit and replace it with a holy one. If you choose pornography, choose for one week to substitute time with the Scriptures for that unhealthy time. If you have friends who take you to places that lead you into sinfulness or wasteful behavior, sign up for a service team or a prayer group that meets at the exact same time. If you are addicted to cigarettes, find a partner who will encourage you in giving those up and spend time with you when the worst withdrawals and temptations come. If you overeat, find a way to spend time at a gym or walking with friends at a time of day that you normally are tempted to snack.

5. Grow in contentment for who you are, what you have, and who God is. Memorize the following verses and recite them throughout the day when temptation to lose self-control threatens you:

> For I have learned to be content with whatever I have. I know what it is to have little, and I know what it is to have plenty. In any and all circumstances, I have learned the secret of being well-fed and of going hungry, of having plenty and of being in need. I can do all things through Christ who strengthens me.
>
> PHILIPPIANS 4:11-13 NRSV

6. Learn the simple prayer: "Jesus, you are enough. Thank you. Amen." Use this prayer regularly throughout the day and most often when temptations or habits overwhelm you.

Conclusions and Suggestions

"...the fruit of the Spirit is love, joy, peace, patience, kindness, goodness, faithfulness, gentleness, self-control..."

God has much in store for each one of us. He has high hopes and big dreams for our lives. Desiring to bless us in every way, He invites you and me to a new way of life. He wants to help us leave behind the corruption and disappointments of this world to become a fruit-full follower of His Son. The Holy Spirit stands waiting for each of us.

What an opportunity lies before you and me! What possibilities! In Christ, you and I have an invitation to: a life full of love, joy, and peace; a life bearing patience, kindness, and goodness; a life rich in faithfulness, gentleness, and self-control. And we will discover that the fruit of God's Spirit all complement one another so that the more one grows, the more the others will grow too. After all, each of the fruit come from the same Spirit, God's Spirit. And best of all, the more we mature in Christ, the more our lives will bear a rich harvest of God's fruit.

I pray that you will seize the opportunity and take the steps to allow God's grace to make your life completely new. Even more, I pray that God will mold you into the person He desires you to be—a follower of Jesus bearing fruit in every aspect of your life. The suggestions and tips included in this book are designed to help you do just that.

It is very simple. The words of Peter are a reminder that Jesus invites you to enter His eternal kingdom which He has richly provided. Enjoy!

His divine power has given us everything needed for life and godliness, through the knowledge of Him who called us by His own glory and goodness. Thus, He has given us, through these things, His precious and very great promises, so that through them you may escape from the corruption that is in the world because of lust and *may become participants of the divine nature.* For this very reason, you must make every effort to support your faith with goodness, and goodness with knowledge, and knowledge with self-control, and self-control with endurance, and endurance with godliness, and godliness with mutual affection, and mutual affection with love. For if these things are yours and are increasing among you, they keep you from being ineffective and *unfruitful* in the knowledge of our Lord Jesus Christ. For anyone who lacks these things is near-sighted and blind, and is forgetful of the cleansing of past sins. Therefore, brethren, be all the more eager to confirm your call and election, for if you do this, you will never stumble. *For in this way, entry into the eternal kingdom of our Lord and Savior Jesus Christ will be richly provided for you.*

2 Peter 1:3-11

Study Questions

Introduction
1. Memorize Galatians 5:22-23. Name the nine fruit of the Spirit.
2. What is the difference between spiritual fruit and spiritual gifts?
3. How can we have these spiritual fruit in our lives?
4. Why does the author state that after receiving the gift of a new life in Jesus, "We have changed. No, we have *been* changed."?
5. How will the world know we belong to Jesus?

Love
1. What is another name for God's love?
2. In your own words, how would you define *agape* love?
3. How is *agape* love different from other types of love that we experience?
4. What is meant by the phrase "love is vertical"?
5. Why is it important that God loves us first?
6. What is meant by the phrase "love is horizontal"?
7. Read Luke 10:25-37. In what ways does the Samaritan exhibit *agape* love?
8. Read Mark 10:17-22. In what ways does Jesus exhibit *agape* love?
9. How is it possible to lavish *agape* love on someone and still have them go away sad?
10. How then can Christians "love one another with recklessness"?
11. Explain the sentence, "We have *agape* love in our lives only because God has shown His love for us in Jesus."

12. Name some practical examples of a love that will "cost us something."

13. How does the NIV translation of 1 John 4:12 help us to understand the biblical concept of perfection?

Joy

1. The author writes, "While negativism is highly contagious, joy is not so contagious," and, therefore, "joy must be cultivated." Why do you think this is true in our world?

2. In Luke 2:10, the angel said, "I bring you good news of great joy for all people." How would you explain this "good news of great joy" to someone who did not understand?

3. How does Jesus bring joy to your life?

4. Part of the joy that Jesus brings to our lives is a *freedom* that is made possible by the empty tomb. How does Jesus' resurrection give us freedom?

5. The original Greek meaning of the word "rejoice" in 1 Peter 8:9 is "to leap for joy, exult, to show one's joy by leaping and skipping." What is it that we're supposed to be this joyful about? Is this your response? Why or why not?

6. From the parable of the talents in Matthew 25, how do we enter into the joy of our master?

7. What practical ways do you try to combat the truism "negative people breed negative people" in your own life? In the lives of your children?

Peace

1. Where do you need peace?

2. Finding peace with God is the first priority in our lives. How do we do this?

3. When we live in Jesus, we acquire peace, and that peace not only lives in us, it *protects* us. Can you give an example of this from your experience?

4. Why must we first have peace with God before we can have peace with ourselves?

5. In spiritual terms, who are you? What does this understanding have to do with peace in your life?

6. What is the difference between the spiritual fruit of peace in your life and the peace that one may get from transcendental meditation?

7. Read Romans 12:14-18. How does being at peace with God and at peace with ourselves allow us to live out these commands?

8. Read Matthew 5:9. We are called to be *active* not passive in our peace relationships with others. Give examples of how we can "practice peace."

9. How does peace begin in our prayers?

Patience

1. There may be as many common sayings about patience as any other desired quality. List several.

2. What biblical examples can you think of that demonstrate God's patience?

3. How has God been patient with you in your own life?

4. The author describes three different kinds of patience. The first is end-time patience. How would you describe this in your own words?

5. Because we Christians know the outcome of history, how should we live differently than the world lives?

6. Read Hebrews 6:10-12. What role does trust play in developing kingdom patience in our lives?

7. Describe social patience.

8. Why does social patience blossom directly out of end-time patience?

9. "Bearing with one another," or social patience, is often linked with the ability to forgive. Explain this relationship.

10. How is the third type, personal endurance and patience, different from the other two types?

11. How can God use suffering in our lives for our ultimate good?

12. God grows patience in every believer's life. In what part of your life is this truth most noticeable?

Kindness

1. Our natural disposition toward others is to view them as less important or valuable than ourselves. What trends have you noticed in our culture that bear this out?

2. Without digging too deep, give an example from your own life in the last week of how this principle has proven true.

3. A few verses before Ephesians 2:7, Paul makes reference to those who live "in the passions of our flesh, carrying out the desires of the body and the mind, and were by nature children of wrath." How is it possible to view those in our society who may fit that description as equal to or more important than yourself? Why is it critical to be able to see the "unlovable" in that light?

4. What do you think God's usual frame of mind is towards you? Toward the world?

5. Read Romans 2:1-4 again. If we truly show no condemnation of those around us, manifesting the fruit of God's kindness, how might that entice someone to repentance?

6. Evangelism has been described as "one beggar showing another beggar where to find bread." Why might a hungry beggar be more receptive to the gospel when handed to him from another beggar, as opposed to a handout from another source?

7. Who are the people around you who may look up to you? How can you be another "beggar" to them?

8. Describe the kindness of Jesus with His disciples.

9. Why does it take "courage to be kind," as the author states?

10. Review 1 Peter 2:1-3. What may turn a good action into a righteous action?

11. One can easily be envious of those who have more "stuff." How does God see those folks, and how might looking at them through His lens help our attitude?

Goodness

1. What happens when we "miss the mark"?

2. What are the three ways Jesus uses mercy to teach about goodness?

3. When we sin, rather than "sentence us to death," what does God do? Why?

4. What lies at the heart of being a Christian? Why does that make sense?

5. How is the world viewed through God's eyes? Why is it so hard for us to do likewise?

6. If "giving is joy," as the author states, why is it so difficult for us to give joyfully?

7. Compare life lived in the flesh vs. life lived in the Spirit. Which would you prefer? Why?

Faithfulness

1. What is the first image that comes to mind when you say the word "faithful"? Why?

2. What does it mean to be a faithful employee?

3. What are the attributes that describe a faithful God?

4. Romans 4:21 says that Abraham was "fully convinced that God was able to do what He had promised." List several biblical promises God has made to us as believers.

5. Faithfulness means trusting God, and is the foundation of our Christian walk. How can we grow in our ability to trust the Lord?

6. Read Matthew 25:14-30 again. The master, representing God, confronts the third servant who views the master as a "hard man" and was terrified of him, wanting only to run from him. What might lead someone to feel that way about God?

7. How might one minister to that person?

8. The master entrusted great wealth to all three servants. What are the four examples the author gives of ways God gifts us?

9. Name two ways you could better manage the time God has entrusted to you?

10. We all have some talent or special ability with which God has gifted us. Think of yours, and how you could better use that talent to glorify Him.

11. List the two examples the author cites of ways we can glorify God and produce a return on His investment in us.

12. Again, referring to the parable of the talents, the author states, "God encourages His people to take risks to share the gospel." Give an example of when the Holy Spirit has nudged you in this regard. Why do we sometimes resist these promptings?

13. There is an element of perseverance in faithfulness. How did Carl demonstrate this? How is such perseverance possible?

14. Carl had a deep loyalty to Christ. Would you describe yourself as loyal to the Savior? Prayerfully turn to the Lord, asking Him to grow loyalty, trustworthiness, and faithfulness in you.

Gentleness

1. What images in our culture come to mind with the words "gentleness" or "meekness"?

2. Some have described biblical gentleness as a wild horse that has been tamed or brought under control. How might this example apply to your Christian walk?

3. Biblical gentleness is a character trait that can come only from God. Read Acts 22:3-10 and describe in your own words the almost instantaneous change in Paul's character toward gentleness.

4. Sometimes we can understand a concept better by seeing an example of the opposite. Read John 18:8-11. How is Peter not displaying biblical gentleness in this passage?

5. How does Jesus epitomize biblical gentleness in John 19:7-11?

6. How is biblical meekness a sign of strength?

7. What is the relationship between gentleness and humility?

8. Do you agree that "the world is full of arrogant, pushy, self-righteous Christians"? Why are all of us at times "eager to point out the sins and failures" of the people around us?

9. Why is a gentle spirit essential in sharing your faith with non-believers?

10. Do you know of any "310-year-old grudges"? How can God's growing spirit of gentleness in a believer begin the restoration process?

11. Using the example of Joseph, the author writes that God shaped his spirit with such gentleness that Joseph is able to tell his brothers, "So it was not you who sent me into Egypt but God." How can your gentle spirit help other Christians to grow deeper in their faith?

12. True or false: "Godly gentleness means never getting angry." Explain your answer.

13. At least three of the author's "Tips" suggest a mind-body connection that could impact one's spirit of gentleness. Have you seen this in your own life?

Self Control

1. Self control is listed as the last of the fruit of the Spirit. Why would it be a good candidate for first?

2. Why is it the hardest fruit to enjoy?

3. List the six biblical steps toward self-control. Apply them to your life.

4. What are the priorities in your life?

5. What is "spiritual marrow"? Why is it so important?

6. What is the key to self-control?

For additional copies of this book please contact:
Resource Center
Mount Pisgah
9820 Nesbit Ferry Road
Alpharetta, GA 30022
678.336.3148
resourcecenter@mountpisgah.org

Discounts available for orders of 10 or more.